A QUESTION OF SPORT

Do you ever watch this quiz and think you could do better than the team of sports professionals in front of you?

Now you can find out without leaving home. Every sports fan – young and old – will enjoy puzzling his or her way through this selection of hundreds of questions from the popular BBC tv series. Whether you're a specialist, or just generally interested in sport, there's a quiz to suit you here. And if you're really stumped, the answers are at the back.

A QUESTION OF SPORT

**Questions and answers from the
BBC tv quiz game**

Hazel Lewthwaite

Illustrated by Alan Burton

BBC/KNIGHT BOOKS

Copyright © British Broadcasting Corporation 1984
Illustrations copyright © British Broadcasting Corporation 1984

*First published 1984 by the British Broadcasting
Corporation/Knight Books*

British Library C.I.P.

Lewthwaite, Hazel
  A question of sport.
  1. Sports – Juvenile literature
  I. Title
  796'.076   GV706.8

  ISBN 0 340 34510 1

      0 563 20266 1(BBC)

Printed and bound in Great Britain for the British
Broadcasting Corporation, 35 Marylebone High Street,
London W1M 4AA and Hodder and Stoughton
Paperbacks, a division of Hodder and Stoughton Ltd.,
Mill Road, Dunton Green, Sevenoaks, Kent (Editorial
Office: 47 Bedford Square, London, WC1 3DP) by
Cox and Wyman Ltd., Reading. Photoset by
Rowland Phototypesetting Ltd.,
Bury St Edmunds, Suffolk.

Contents

Introduction

A Question of Sport first appeared on BBC1 in January 1970, and I've been involved with it from the beginning. I've had the pleasure of producing the programme, and the equal pleasure of setting many of the questions. Not on my own though, for everyone who works on the production team contributes questions, as do several BBC commentators, not least David Coleman, who has been our highly knowledgeable question master for the last five series.

The questions are not designed to trap the panellists. Indeed, we try, as far as possible, to ensure that they are within their field of sporting knowledge, though some have been known to forget things under the pressure of being in a television studio!

The questions in this book are taken mainly from recent series, and have been updated, as far as possible, to September 1983. But as sport never stands still, it's likely that a record or two has been broken since then so please bear with us!

Two of the rounds in the programme itself are 'Home and Away', and 'One-Minute'. 'Home' questions are on a particular sport, and are usually directed at someone with knowledge in that field. 'Away' are general sports questions. The 'One-Minute Round' has five questions to be answered in a minute, and in the book each round has been divided into two lots of five. So anyone who is devising their own sports quiz on the lines of the programme can use the book as a guide. The scoring is: 1 point each for the first two questions; two points for questions 3 and 4; three points for question 5. 'Home' questions normally score 1 point, and 'Away' questions 2 points, but I have included, in both cases, some two- or three-part questions as well, which quiz-makers can use if they want to make things more difficult for their teams!

Obviously, it was not possible, in a book, to give the sort of visual questions we use on the screen, but there are a number of picture questions for you to puzzle over.

Whether you want to set a quiz, or just test your own sporting knowledge, I hope you'll enjoy this book. I hope, too, that you, like millions of others, will go on enjoying *A Question of Sport* on television. A final word to any contestants in the next series: it's no use mugging up the answers in this book before you come to the studio – we'll be setting completely new questions!

Hazel Lewthwaite

1 One-minute Round 1

TEAM A

1 On which course was the 1982 British Open Golf Championship staged?

2 Who were the two French Rugby Union brothers of the 1960s, nicknamed the 'Fleas'?

3 In which two sports did these people make their name: Bobby-Joe Morrow, Jeanette Altweg?

4 Two men dead-heated for the 1982 Commonwealth Games 200-Metres Gold Medal. Who were they?

5 Complete these World Cup finalists:
    1982   Italy v ....
    1978   West Germany v ....
    1974   Argentina v ....

TEAM B

1 Where were the 1982 Commonwealth Games staged?

2 Which is the only nation to have achieved four Olympic Team Gold Medals in the modern Pentathlon?

3 Complete these famous pairs:
    Towler and ....
    Dixon and ....

4 Which horse and rider won the 1982 Grand National?

5 What are the married names of these tennis players: a) B. J. Moffitt, b) M. Smith, c) M. Simionescu?

2   Home: Soccer 1

1 Three players have scored in two separate World Cup Final games. Who are they?

2 Four men have twice been named 'Footballer of the Year' by the Football Writers' Association. Can you identify two of them?

3 Who is the only Liverpool player to score for the club in two FA Cup Finals?

4 Which player achieved the same feat for Spurs in the 1961 and 1962 FA Cup Finals?

5 Who captained Aston Villa when they won the European Cup in 1982?

6 In the 1979 Cup Final between Arsenal and Manchester United, three goals were scored in the last four minutes. Who were the scorers?

7 Which player scored in both Celtic's European Cup Final appearances in 1967 and 1970?

8 Three one-million-pound players joined Manchester City between September 1979 and September 1981. Who were they?

9 Alan Simonsen scored against Liverpool in the 1977 European Cup Final. For which club was he playing?

10 Apart from Liverpool in the 1977 match, two other English clubs have conceded goals in the European Cup Final. Who are they?

11 Which player scored all five goals in England's 5–0 defeat of Cyprus in 1975?

12 Which club has reached the FA Cup Final seven times, and won on every occasion?

Which Club?

Which football clubs wear these badges?

a

e

c

d

e

f

3   Home: Athletics 1

1 In 1896, Edwin H. Flack won the Olympic 800-Metres and 1500-Metres Double. Only one man has ever achieved that feat since. Who was he?

2 In the 1976 Olympics, the British team won only one medal on the track. Who was the lone medallist?

3 The women's 200-Metres in the 1974 Commonwealth Games in Christchurch brought an Australian girl her fourth Commonwealth Games Gold Medal. Who was she?

4 Four years later in Edmonton, the 200-Metres Gold went to another Australian. Who was she?

5 Which pole-vaulter took that Gold Medal at the Mexico Olympics?

6 Four years later in Munich, that pole-vaulter cleared exactly the same height, but this time it was only good enough for Silver. Who took the Gold?

7 In September 1979, Pietro Mennea of Italy set a new World record for the 200-Metres. It had taken eleven years to beat the previous one – set by whom?

8 Since the 400-Metres became a women's Olympic event in 1964, two British girls have won Silver Medals in it. Who are they?

9 Only one Russian athlete has won an Olympic Gold Medal in the decathlon. Who is he?

10 The oldest competitor to break an athletics World record in a standard Olympic event, was a woman javelin thrower married to a famous distance runner. Who was she?

11 Which world-class English athlete retired from competitive racing in 1978, with a full set of European Medals, a Commonwealth Gold and an Olympic Silver to his name?

12 What unique record does Diane Leather hold?

4 Home: Horse Racing 1

1 Henry Cecil's first classic success, as a trainer, was in winning the 1975 2,000-Guineas with the 33–1 outsider Bolkonski. Who was the jockey?

2 Where is the Lincolnshire Handicap run?

3 In 1981, Spindrifter equalled a record of thirteen victories by a two-year-old in a season. Which horse already held the record?

4 Which race-course, now closed, used to be nicknamed 'The Frying Pan'?

5 In 1982, Golden Fleece became the first winner of an English classic sired by Nijinsky, but Nijinsky had previously sired a winner of the King George VI and Queen Elizabeth Stakes. Can you identify the horse?

6 Lester Piggott had his first Derby win in 1954. On which horse?

7 Which jockey won the first-ever Ladies' race in this country?

8 It's no exaggeration to say that this horse has influenced National Hunt breeding more than any other horse in history. Bred in France in 1943, he has sired, in Ireland, three Grand National winners and the Cheltenham Gold Cup winner The Dikler. What was his name?

9 The Schweppes Gold Trophy started in 1963. In the first two years, the race was won by the same horse and jockey. Who were they?

10 One horse dominated flat-racing in 1952, winning the Derby, the King George VI and Queen Elizabeth Stakes, the Eclipse Stakes and the St Leger. What was he called?

11 Which two English classics are restricted to fillies?

12 Cottage Rake won the Cheltenham Gold Cup three years in succession (1948–49–50). Which was the next horse to achieve a hat-trick in this race?

5   Away 1

1 In what sport, other than soccer, might you find Crystal Palace meeting Sunderland at Wembley?

2 What is 'Hell's Half-Acre'?

3 Although it began in America just after the turn of the century, this sport found its true beginnings in Australia in 1923. Five years later it reached this country, taking place for the first time in Epping Forest. Today, it attracts a large following, with its most successful world champions having come from Sweden and New Zealand. What is the sport?

4 An invitation event in Texas in 1977 provided the first unofficial world title in women's modern penthathlon. Who was the winner?

5 If you've passed Curzon, travelled through Brabazon, yet still have to pass Nani's Bridge, where are you?

6 Why did Neroli Fairhall create history at the 1982 Commonwealth Games?

7 In which knock-out competition, in 1982, did St Fagans beat Collingham and take the trophy back to Wales?

8 In which sport is the order of play determined by stringing or lagging?

9 In 1957, this girl was one of Britain's top table tennis stars and reached all three Finals in the World Championships. She lost all three matches, but went on to greater fame in another sport. Who is she?

10 Arthur Milton was England's last dual international – in which sports?

11 In which sport is the Palma Match contested?

12 The Earl of Winchilsea, Lord Charles Lennox, the Duke of York and the Duke of Dorset founded one of our sporting institutions. Which one?

Who's This?

Can you identify the writers of these famous autographs?

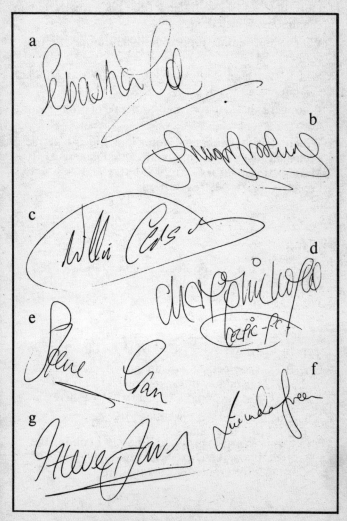

6   One-minute Round 2

TEAM A

1 Only one side beat Ireland, the 1982 Rugby Union champions. Which one?

2 Which show jumper topped the 1982 European money-winners' list?

3 Which two men contested the 1982 World Snooker Championship Final?

4 Who were the first two men to break the four-minute mile?

5 Which British swimmers won Gold Medals in these events at the 1982 Commonwealth Games: a) 100-Metres Breast Stroke, b) 200-Metres and 400-Metres Freestyle, c) 200-Metres Butterfly?

TEAM B

1 Which was the last Football League club managed by Jock Stein before he became manager of Scotland?

2 Who partnered Bobby Schwartz to the speedway World Pairs Championship in December 1982?

3 Floor exercises and beam are two of the disciplines in women's Olympic gymnastics. What are the other two?

4 One British competitor won an individual Silver Medal at the 1972 Olympics, and an individual Bronze Medal at the 1976 Olympics. Who is he, and what was his event?

5 Fill in the missing Derby-winning jockeys:
  a) 1971 Mill Reef ridden by ....?
  b) 1975 Grundy ridden by ....?
  c) 1979 Troy ridden by ....?

Wimbledon Winners

Bjorn Borg defeated four men in Wimbledon Singles Finals, but in his Wimbledon career, he himself was also defeated four times. Can you identify the four victors, and the four vanquished?

7   Home: Cricket 1

1 Who was the first player in England to score 1000 runs and take 100 wickets in limited-over cricket?

2 In the 1972 Test series against Australia, John Edrich opened the England innings in all five Tests, but with three different partners. Who were they?

3 In 1956, Jim Laker took 19 wickets in a Test match – which remains a record. Since then, one man has come within three wickets of equalling that record. Who was he?

4 The first World Cup Final was at Lords in 1975. Who were the finalists?

5 In the same year, who were the beaten Semi-finalists?

6 The Australian equivalent to our County Championship is a shield, named after an English city which has also staged Test and County cricket. Can you name it?

7 In 1959, who, at the age of fifteen, had the distinction of becoming the youngest-ever Test cricketer?

8 Who, in 1979, became the first man to score a century in the final of the Benson and Hedges Cup?

9 Which was the first minor county to beat a major county in the Gillette (now NatWest) Cup?

10 Which New Zealander captained his country from 1956 to 1965?

11 Which is the only team to win the Benson and Hedges Cup three times?

12 What was exceptional about the Golden Jubilee Test match between England and Australia at Lords, on 4 August 1976?

8 Home: Swimming and Diving

1 Which Briton won both the Highboard and Springboard Diving titles at the 1978 Commonwealth Games?

2 Which Australian, in 1964, became the first swimmer to win the same Olympic title at three successive Games?

3 Which diver made his international debut at thirteen, was a European champion at 14, and won four Gold Medals in three Commonwealth Games?

4 A new stroke first had its own event in Olympic competition in 1956. What was it?

5 Shane Gould won the 200-Metres Freestyle at the Munich Olympics in a World record time, beating the former World record holder into second place as well. Which girl came second?

6 At which Olympics did Anita Lonsborough win her Gold Medal and in which event?

7 Which diver won the Highboard event at three successive Olympic Games?

8 Two men dominated the 200-Metres Breast Stroke event at both the Munich and Montreal Olympics, winning Gold and Silver on both occasions. Who were they?

9 Who is the only British girl to have won an Olympic medal in Springboard Diving?

10 In 1968, which girl became the first to win three individual Gold Medals at one Olympic Games?

11 Who, in the 1950s, became the first swimmer to achieve a hat-trick of Olympic, Commonwealth and European Gold Medals?

12 In 1972 which man retained in Munich the two individual Backstroke titles which he had won in the Mexico Olympics in 1968?

9   Home: Boxing 1

1 Which British boxer held the World Welterweight title from December 1975 to June 1976?

2 From whom did this boxer win the title?

3 Who was the first British boxer to win a Lonsdale Belt outright?

4 Who was the first Olympic boxing Gold Medallist to go on to win the World Professional Heavyweight title?

5 Which British boxer was European Featherweight Champion from July 1963 to October 1967 – the longest period of time a British boxer has held a European title?

6 Who was the last Briton to fight for the World Heavyweight title?

7 In 1977, which boxer won the British Middleweight title, after it had been declared vacant owing to Alan Minter's European title commitments?

8 In March 1980, Sugar Ray Leonard successfully defended his World Welterweight crown against a British boxer. Who was he?

9 Three months later, Leonard lost his title – to whom?

10 When Carlos Monzon retired in 1977, who won the vacant World Middleweight title?

11 Muhammed Ali is the only heavyweight boxer in history to have won the title three times. Can you name the three reigning champions whom he defeated?

12 Who is the only boxer, at any weight, to win a World title five times?

Six times Three

Only six riders have won both the two great Three-day Events, at Badminton and Burleigh. Who are they?

10   Away: 2

1 In which sport is 'dunking' a method of scoring?

2 A 24-year-old Californian called Bobbi Hunter made speedway history at Wembley arena in November 1982. Why?

3 In which sport do they compete for the Russell Cargill trophy?

4 In the 1980 Winter Olympics, while her brother was winning a record five Gold Medals, she collected a Bronze and found consolation during the same year by winning the Ladies' World Amateur Road Race cycling title. Who is she?

5 When Australia and New Zealand play their traditional Manning Cup fixture, what is the sport involved?

6 The World Waterskiing Championships have been held twice in Great Britain. At which venue were they held?

7 This game was first recorded as being played between the Turks and the Persians in 600 BC: there are four players each side, competing over periods lasting 7 minutes, and the aim is to score goals. What is the name of this sport?

8 It takes two to twizzle, to choctaw and to mohawk. Why?

9 What is the next colour in the following sequence: white, yellow, orange, green, blue, brown.

10 Can you name the three men who won the Modern Pentathlon Gold Medal for Britain at the Montreal Olympics?

11 With which sport would you associate Caroline Cherry, Flowering Crabapple and Yellow Jasmine?

12 In which sport was Australian Rhonda Thorne the 1982 Ladies' World Champion?

11　　One-minute Round 3

TEAM A

1 Who was the last British athlete to win an Olympic Gold Medal in a Hurdles race?

2 What nationality is motor-cyclist Randy Mamola?

3 In which sports have these people represented their countries?
　　a) Hans Peter Ferner, b) Thomas Smid.

4 Which were the last two non-League clubs to be elected to the Football League?

5 These famous sportswomen married famous sportsmen. Who are their husbands? a) Anita Lonsborough, b) Marion Coakes, c) Ann Packer.

TEAM B

1 Which English club won the European Cup-Winners' Cup in 1971 – the last one to do so?

2 Which famous English horse race was first run in 1776?

3 In which events did these two win Commonwealth Games Gold Medals in 1982? a) Christina Boxer, b) Robert Weir.

4 Two pairs of tennis-playing brothers – what are their surnames?
　　a) Tim and Tom ....?
　　b) Sandy and Gene ....?

5 On which English courses were these British Open victories achieved? a) 1967 Roberto de Vicenzo, b) 1969 Tony Jacklin, c) 1981 Bill Rogers.

12 Home: Soccer 2

1 Two men each scored twice in successive Cup Finals, in 1974 and 1975. Who were they?

2 Who captained Liverpool when they won the European Cup in 1981?

3 Peter Shilton joined Southampton in August 1982. Can you recall his three previous clubs?

4 Which British club won the UEFA Cup in 1981?

5 The 1977, League Cup Final went to a second replay before being decided. Which two teams were involved?

6 The Final of the 1977 League Cup was, of course, at Wembley, but on which grounds were the replays staged?

7 Which player figured in the most expensive transfer deal from a Scottish to an English club?

8 Only two current First Division managers have twice led their clubs to FA Cup Final victories. Who are they?

9 In the 1980 European Cup Winners' Cup, which British team was beaten 5–4 on penalties, after extra time, and by whom?

10 Which player earned the nickname 'Super-Sub' while playing for Liverpool?

11 Who was the leading goal-scorer in the 1978 World Cup Finals?

12 Which player scored the only goal of the game in three FA Cup Semi-finals, for the same club, between 1965 and 1973 – and each time ended up at Wembley on the losing side?

13   Home: Tennis 1

1 In the 1982 US Open, both singles events were won by Americans, and both runners-up came from the same country: what is its name?

2 The 1977 Wimbledon Men's Doubles Final was an all-Australian affair. Can you name the eventual winners?

3 In 1981, John McEnroe won both the Men's Singles and Doubles at Wimbledon. Who was the last man to achieve that feat before him?

4 Billie-Jean King won the Wimbledon Ladies' Singles six times. Who was the only woman she beat twice in the Final?

5 Who was the first man to achieve the Grand Slam twice?

6 Who was the first British player to win a Wimbledon Singles title after the war?

7 Billie-Jean King won the Mixed Doubles at Wimbledon four times, with the same partner. Who was he?

8 Can you name the other three players who were in the victorious Wightman Cup squad in 1978, with Virginia Wade and Sue Barker?

9 Maria Bueno won the Wimbledon Singles three times. Can you name the players she defeated in those Finals?

10 John Newcombe won the last Amateur Singles at Wimbledon in 1967. Which German star faced him in the Final?

11 Doris Hart won the Wimbledon Singles in 1951. In the Final, she beat the doubles partner with whom she won the Wimbledon Doubles three years in succession. Whom did she beat?

12 A British pair won the Wimbledon Women's Doubles in 1955. Who were they?

14 Home: Motor Racing

1 Which Grand Prix was staged for several years at Zolder?

2 Who was the first United States driver to win the World Drivers' Championship?

3 Two British drivers became World Champion during the 1970s. Who were they?

4 Eight years on, and almost 12 miles shorter, a circuit returns to the Grand Prix calendar in 1984. Which one?

5 Partnered by Britain's Derek Bell, he came out of retirement to register a record fifth win in the 1981 Le Mans 24-hour race. Who is he?

6 The World Drivers' Championship began in 1950. Who was the first holder of the title?

7 Kyalami is the setting of the South African Grand Prix now, but where was its previous home?

8 Which British driver won the Monaco Grand Prix five times in the 1960s?

9 Only one New Zealander has ever won the World Drivers' Championship. Who was that?

10 The Le Mans 24-hour race was won three times by the same team – in 1958, 1961 and 1962. Who were they?

11 Since the war, the British Grand Prix has been staged on three circuits. Can you name them?

12 In 1982, Keke Rosberg became World Champion, yet he won only one Grand Prix that season. Which one did he win?

Speedway Special

Between 1976 and 1978, Malcolm Simmons recorded a hat-trick of wins in speedway's World Pairs Championship. He had three different partners: can you name them?

15   Away 3

1 Since their inception in 1924, the Winter Olympics have been staged three times in the USA, at two venues. Can you name the venues?

2 The name of this sport comes from the Dutch word meaning 'to hunt' or 'chase'. The first recorded contest in this country was between two kings – Charles II and his brother, later James II. Since then, Britain has had a good deal of success in the sport, including Gold Medals in the Mexico, Munich and Montreal Olympics. What is the sport?

3 In which sport do contestants score marks for their ability at a three, an eight, a loop and a rocker?

4 In what Olympic sport do you have two sets of 36 at 90, 2 at 70, 2 at 50, and 2 at 30?

5 For what sporting event do you pass through the Doherty Gates?

6 Which sport is to be re-introduced to the Olympics in 1988, after a 64-year absence?

7 Which country collected its first-ever Gold Medal at the Moscow Olympics, and for which sport?

8 This is a comparatively new sport, which gets its name from the Spanish word for a diving board. Three of the terms used in it are 'Miller', 'Randolph' and 'Kaboom'. What is it?

9 In which sport would you encounter the 'Hell of the North'?

10 His father was a singer, his mother an actress, his sister shot JR, and he won the US Amateur Golf Championship. Can you name the family?

11 In which sport would you find an 'Eskimo roll'?

12 What is unusual about the Bobby Jones Golf Classic, held every year in the Detroit suburb of Tyrone Hills?

16   One-minute Round 4

TEAM A

1 Martina Navratilova won the 1982 Wimbledon Women's Doubles. Who was her partner?

2 Where is the venue for the World Professional Snooker Championships?

3 The Kop is at Anfield, but where would you find the Hill and the Chair?

4 Which two counties last shared cricket's County Championship?

5 In which sports are the following terms used? a) double axel, b) massé, c) tsukahara.

TEAM B

1 Where is the US Masters Golf Tournament always played?

2 In which city did Aston Villa win the 1982 European Cup Final?

3 Which countries do these tennis players represent? a) Guillermo Vilas, b) Vitas Gerulaitis.

4 Can you name two of Britain's 4 × 100-Metres Women's Relay team, which won a Bronze Medal at the Moscow Olympics?

5 Which famous sports stars are known by these nicknames? a) Crazy Horse, b) Crafty Cockney, c) White Lightning.

17   Home: Athletics 2

1 In the 3000-Metres steeplechase at the Mexico Olympics, a Kenyan athlete, running in his first steeplechase, won the Gold Medal, with one of his fellow countrymen coming second. Who were the two athletes?

2 Kenya repeated this feat four years later, in 1972, with two different runners winning Gold and Silver. Who are they?

3 Which British athlete broke the World record for the 10,000-Metres in 1973?

4 In three successive Olympic Games – in 1952, 1956 and 1960 – Britain's women High-Jumpers won Silver Medals. Can you name the three girls?

5 The Women's 1500-Metres was run for the first time at the Munich Olympics. Who won that first Gold Medal?

6 Who was the first British woman to win a Gold Medal in an Olympic track event?

7 Jesse Owens' world long jump record stood for 25 years. Who finally broke it?

8 Ron Clarke, for all his World records, never won an Olympic race. The best he managed was a Bronze in the 10,000-Metres – in which Olympics?

9 Which British athlete won the Decathlon Gold Medal in the 1974 Commonwealth Games?

10 Who was the only British athlete to win track medals in both the Commonwealth and European Games in 1978?

11 Two Italian athletes have won Olympic Gold Medals in the Men's 200-Metres. Who are they?

12 Since the war, Britain has collected only three medals, none of them Gold, in the Olympic 5000-Metres. Who were the successful runners?

Backwards to Victory

Can you name three sports which you win (or lose!) when going backwards?

This is a border-line case, because you go forwards and backwards in the Fosbury Flop!

18   Home: Rugby Union 1

1 France won the Grand Slam in 1977 – but what were the two unique achievements by the French during that season?

2 In 1977, to celebrate the Queen's Silver Jubilee, a unique match was staged at Twickenham. One side was the Barbarians. Which was the other?

3 Who was the sole Irish representative playing in that unique match?

4 In 1976, Scotland beat England to take the Calcutta Cup. Who captained Scotland that day?

5 Which French International player enjoyed the nickname (first given to Napoleon) of 'The Little Corporal'?

6 Three Llanelli players were ever-present in the 1976 Welsh Grand Slam side. One was the legendary Phil Bennett. Who were the other two?

7 When the Barbarians played the East Midlands in 1979, an injury to Dusty Hare resulted in an ex-England international (who originally turned up to watch) taking the field. Who was it?

8 During the British Isles tour of New Zealand in 1977, three replacements were called for – one English, and two Welsh. Who were they?

9 Who was the first Maori to captain the All Blacks?

10 The first Rugby Union Club Championship was contested at Twickenham in 1972. Who were the two finalists?

11 The career of Gareth Edwards spanned fifty-three consecutive internationals (from 1967–78). During that time, he was substituted twice – once in 1970, once in 1973. Who were the two players involved?

12 Which two teams annually contest the Mobbs Memorial Trophy?

19   Home: Snooker 1

1 In 1978, the Welsh mining village of Tredegar achieved a unique double in the world of snooker. What was that distinction?

2 In the first State Express World Team Classic in 1979, Perrie Mans was in the Rest of the World team, with another South African, and an Irishman. Who were they?

3 The following year, Mans was again in the team, but with a Scotsman and an American. Who were they?

4 In the 1982 World Championships, Willie Thorne reached the Quarter-Finals, defeating two former World champions on the way. Who were they?

5 Who, in 1980, became the youngest player ever to win the World Amateur title?

6 The World Snooker Championship has only once been staged outside this country. Where was it held?

7 At the ripe age of fifty-four, the legendary Joe Davis recorded a First for himself – and for snooker. What was it?

8 Cliff Thornburn won the World Championship in 1980, but he also lost a World Championship final before that – to whom?

9 Who was the only man to hold, simultaneously, both snooker and billiards World titles?

10 Who took the first-ever Professional Players' title in 1982?

11 Doug Mountjoy made 145, the highest break of the 1982 World Championship. Who was he playing at the time?

12 What is the minimum number of snooker balls required to achieve a century break?

Gold Beaters

The first five horses past thc post in the 1983 Cheltenham Gold Cup were all trained by Michael Dickinson. Can you name them?

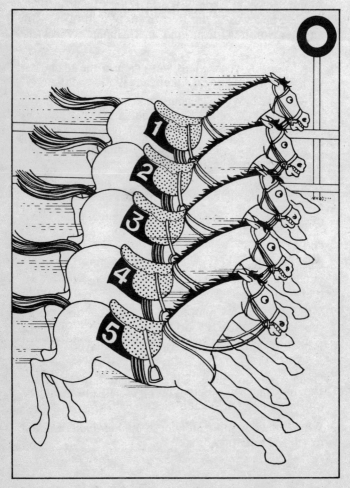

20   Away 4

1 This game was first called 'Gossima', and enjoyed a world-wide craze in the 1890s, as a children's toy, and as an after-dinner pastime. It suffered a decline, except as a children's game, but was revived in the 1920s, and is now played all over the world. Britain has had no World champion since 1954, but did boast a male European champion in 1981, and a female European champion in 1976. To which sport does this refer?

2 Can you name two current Olympic sports in which men compete against women as individuals?

3 Blue and black are always partners against red and yellow, and the game is won or lost on the return journey: what is it?

4 In which sport do competitors engage in 'souping'?

5 Whom did 18-year-old John Dunne beat at Coatbridge early in 1982, to cause a major upset in his sport?

6 In which sport was Britain's Frankie Wainman the 1979 World Champion, winning his title at the White City?

7 Gordon Pirie was the first-ever British champion at this sport, in 1967, and retained his title the following year. What is it?

8 A man, better-known outside sport, was runner-up in the 1979 Le Mans 24-hour race. Who was he?

9 At which game did the Brewers' Shades beat the Ifield Musketeers at Tinsley Green in Sussex to win the 1978 World Championship?

10 In the 1920s, a walker and a rider entered which sport?

11 The assassination of a famous archduke will be linked with sport in 1984. What is the connection?

12 Where would you be if you fell into the Trout Hatchery?

21   One-minute Round 5

TEAM A

1 Who captained the 1982 Australian Rugby Union Touring team?

2 With which sport do you associate the name Wilt Chamberlain?

3 Can you name the winning partnership in the 1983 Grand National?

4 Of the clubs who have won soccer's League Championship since the war, five are no longer in the First Division. Can you name two of them?

5 Which County cricket sides play at these grounds? a) Edgbaston, b) Grace Road, c) St Lawrence Ground.

TEAM B

1 Where do Ireland play their international Rugby matches?

2 In which sport was Bruce Penhall a World champion?

3 Which two jockeys rode Red Rum on his three Grand National victories?

4 The 1980 Winter Olympics were held at Lake Placid. Where were the two previous venues in 1976 and 1972?

5 With which sports are these governing bodies associated? a) LTA, b) WBC, c) WPBSA.

Which Game?

In which game are these pieces of equipment used?

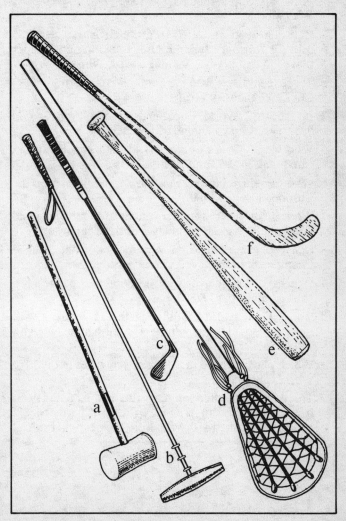

22   Home: Soccer 5

1 A Queen's Park Rangers' player reserved the first goal of his FA Cup career for the 1982 Final at Wembley. Who was he?

2 Between 1966 and 1977, Pat Jennings collected 55 caps for Northern Ireland. Only one other goalkeeper played in that period, winning 6 caps. Who was he?

3 Three teams have won the Football League (now Milk) Cup three times. Who are they?

4 In the 1982 World Cup Finals, four players scored hat-tricks. Can you name two of them?

5 Who were Celtic's opponents in their two European Cup Finals in 1967 and 1970?

6 Who captained Nottingham Forest when they won the European Cup in 1980?

7 Who, in 1974, was the first winner of the Professional Footballers' Association Player of the Year award?

8 Can you name two clubs who have won the League Championship three years in succession?

9 Which Watford player was the Football League's top goal-scorer in the 1978–9 season?

10 Roger Hunt had a scintillating ten-year career with Liverpool, but left them in 1969 to finish his career with which club?

11 Which player scored in all Brazil's matches in the 1970 World Cup Finals?

12 Three months after winning the FA Cup in 1978, Ipswich returned to Wembley for the Charity Shield and were thrashed 5–0. Who were their conquerors?

23   Home: Cricket 2

1 The 1973 West Indian touring team to England included four Warwickshire players. Can you name them?

2 Who was the first bowler to take 300 Test wickets?

3 Which current international cricketer was also a World Cup footballer?

4 In the 1975 Australia v England series, the England captain dropped himself for the Fourth Test, because of lack of form. His place was taken as captain, for the only time in his career, by one of England's most experienced internationals. Who was he, and who was the dropped captain?

5 Worcestershire have twice been beaten in the Benson and Hedges Cup Final by the same county – which one?

6 Surrey dominated the County Championship in the 1950s with seven wins between 1952 and 1958. Who were their two captains in this period?

7 Which bowler took 14 wickets in a Test Match against England in 1976?

8 He was the first cricketer to take 100 wickets and score 1000 runs in a season, and one of the few cricketers to score a century and take 10 wickets in an innings, in the same match. Who was he?

9 Which was the first County to win the Gillette (now NatWest) Cup and the John Player League in the same season?

10 Who succeeded Don Bradman when he retired as captain of the Australian Test side?

11 In the Third Test in 1977, two England cricketers came together for the first time, one making his debut, the other ending a self-imposed exile. Who were they?

12 Bandula Warnapura and Sidath Wettimuny created history for their country on 17 February 1982. What was the occasion?

24   Home: Golf 1

1 Tom Watson won the British Open for the fifth time in 1983. In this century, two other golfers have equalled this achievement. Who are they?

2 Where would you find the Eden and the Jubilee?

3 Two golfers were involved in a play-off for the 1970 British Open. Who were they?

4 Which player, in his first year as a professional, won the 1982 Bob Hope British Classic?

5 He won the British Open at Troon in 1962, and on the eve of the 1982 Championship on the same course, he was made an honorary life member of the club. Who is he?

6 Which famous golfer, on his forty-fifth birthday, tragically signed for a 4 instead of a 3, during his final round, and lost a major title by one stroke?

7 On the above occasion, which title was at stake, and who was the rather lucky winner?

8 Who is the only left-handed golfer to win the British Open?

9 Which man has won the World Matchplay Championship a record five times?

10 Who were the last two non-Americans to win the British Open?

11 Jack Nicklaus won the 1975 US Masters by one shot, in a dramatic finish. Each of the two players chasing him missed a putt on the 18th to tie the championship with Nicklaus. Who were those two players?

12 Who was the last British golfer to win the British Open, before Tony Jacklin's success in 1969?

British Open

1926 was the last time an American golfer won the British Open at Royal Lytham and St Annes. Who were the six winners there since then?

25   Home: Show Jumping

1 Can you name the British horse and rider who won a Silver Medal in the 1972 Olympic Games?

2 Which famous show jumper won the European Championship in 1968 on Merely-a-Monarch?

3 Eddie Macken took first and second places in the 1976 Hickstead Derby – on which horses?

4 The horse which came second in the 1976 Hickstead Derby had won this race the previous year – but under another name, and with another rider: can you name them?

5 Who was the first rider to win the King George V Gold Cup, on the same horse, three times?

6 Who was the first British show jumper to win the World Championship?

7 A West German rider took the Bronze in the Three-Day Event in the 1964 Olympic Games, and later became famous as a show jumper. Who was he?

8 Two British women riders have won the European Show Jumping Championship more than once. Can you name them?

9 In the 1960 Olympic Games, two brothers took the individual Gold and Silver Medals. Who were they?

10 Who was the first woman to compete in the Olympic Games Show Jumping events?

11 April 1979 saw the conclusion of the first-ever staging of the World Cup. Can you name the winning horse and rider?

12 British riders finished first and second in the 1971 European Ladies Championship. Who were they?

26   Away 5

1 Although he sounds as though he ought to be in hospital, he won a record £115,000 in 1979. Who is he?

2 Since 1928, the Olympic Men's title in this sport was the property of either India or Pakistan, until 1972 when West Germany won the Gold. What is the sport?

3 How did Alexander Belov cause a bit of sporting controversy in 1972?

4 In which sport do countries compete for the Swaythling Cup?

5 Which country won the Swaythling Cup for the twelfth time, in 1979, after a gap of twenty-seven years?

6 Where would you find the most famous Postage Stamp in sport?

7 Which sport was devised, in its modern form, in the hall of a Stately Home, during the reign of Queen Victoria?

8 In which sport do the players use a broom?

9 Since the Winter Olympics began in 1924, which country has won most medals? This country does not win many medals in the Summer Games.

10 There is evidence that this game was played in Ancient Egypt 8000 years ago, and evidence also of its existence in Britain in the first century AD. It also played a part in the victory over Philip of Spain on 19 July 1588. It was 1903 before a full association was set up in England, under the presidency of W. G. Grace. Today, it is a recognised Commonwealth Games sport. What is it?

11 Who was President of the International Olympic Committee before Lord Killanin?

12 She should have been at a graduation ceremony at Rolling Hills High School on 19 August 1981. Instead, she was playing the sport which made her a household name by the age of sixteen. Who is she?

27 One-minute Round 6

TEAM A

1 At which sporting venue would you find Druids?

2 Which bowler has taken most Test match wickets?

3 Only two clubs have won the Football League (now Milk) Cup in successive seasons. Who are they?

4 With which sports do you associate these terms?
    a) tin, b) gulley.

5 Who captained these famous teams?
    a) England's World Cup team in 1966
    b) Britain's Wightman Cup team in 1978
    c) British Lions 1971.

———————————————————

TEAM B

1 At which sporting venue would you find Valentine's?

2 Which batsman has scored most runs in Test cricket?

3 Which two sports are featured in the Olympic Biathlon?

4 With which sports do you associate these terms?
    a) skeet, b) foible.

5 By what nicknames are these sportsmen better known?
    a) Derek Prior Rogers, b) John Thomas Wilson, c) Francis Morgan Thompson.

28   Home: Athletics 3

1 The Olympic Men's 1500-Metres has not been won in a World record time since 1960. Who was the man to achieve it?

2 Can you name the West German javelin thrower who won the Gold Medal in the Women's event at both the Munich and Montreal Olympics?

3 Who won the Gold Medal in the Women's 1500-Metres in the 1978 Commonwealth Games in Edmonton?

4 In the history of the Olympic Games, only one man has ever retained the 5000-Metres title. Can you name him?

5 The Men's 1500-Metres at the 1974 Commonwealth Games was won in a World record time – by whom?

6 Can you name the East German girl who won the Gold Medal in the 400-Metres at the Moscow Olympics?

7 Which Irish athlete took the Silver Medal in the Men's 1500-Metres in the 1978 European Championships?

8 Who was the last girl to win the Olympic sprint double?

9 Parry O'Brien won the Olympic shot put title twice – in 1952 and 1956. He won the Silver in 1960. Who stopped him making it three Gold Medals in a row?

10 In which three events did Mary Rand win medals at the Tokyo Olympics?

11 In the 1974 Commonwealth Games 5000-Metres, Englishmen took the silver and bronze medals. Who were the runners?

12 John Walker of New Zealand won the 1976 Olympic 1500-Metres. Who were the two British runners who reached the Final?

29   Home: Horse Racing 2

1 Who was the last amateur jockey to ride a Champion Hurdle winner?

2 Who was the only National Hunt jockey to ride over 1000 winners?

3 In 1971, Mill Reef won the Derby, the Eclipse Stakes, the King George VI and Queen Elizabeth Stakes and the *Prix de l'Arc de Triomphe*, but finished second in the 2000 Guineas – the only time he was ever beaten in England. Which horse beat him?

4 Who partnered Cut Above in his 1981 St Leger victory at Doncaster?

5 In 1979, the *Prix de l'Arc de Triomphe* was won by the three-year-old filly, Three Troikas. What was the connection betwetween the horse's jockey and trainer?

6 In the 1981 season, two horses were involved in three photo finishes. The races involved were the Irish 2000 Guineas, the Sussex Stakes, and the St James' Palace Stakes. Which were the horses?

7 In 1902, an amazing filly won four out of the five classics, the exception being the Derby. To mark this feat, a race, which is still run, was named after her. Can you name the horse?

8 Peter Easterby trained the first and second horses in the 1981 Cheltenham Gold Cup. Can you name the horses?

9 At the end of the 1969 National Hunt season, two riders tied for the Jockeys' Championship. Who were they?

10 The stallion Northern Dancer has sired two English Derby winners. Can you name them?

11 Josh Gifford rode 122 winners in the 1966–7 National Hunt season. It was six years before the championship was again won with over 100 winners – by whom?

12 Which horse won the English Triple Crown (the Derby, the 2000 Guineas, and the St Leger) in 1970?

Derby Winners

Lester Piggott won the Derby nine times between 1954 and 1983. What were the names of the winning horses?

30   Home: Soccer 4

1 Who scored Aston Villa's only goal in their European Cup Final win in 1982?

2 Who were Aston Villa's opponents in the 1982 European Cup Final?

3 Hungary created a scoring record in the 1982 World Cup with a 10–1 victory – against which team?

4 Ipswich won the UEFA Cup in 1981, but which Scottish side removed them from the tournament in the following season?

5 Malcolm Macdonald played for four clubs in his career. Can you name them?

6 Which Polish player was the top goal-scorer in the 1974 World Cup Finals?

7 Which club appeared in three successive European Cup Winners' Cup Finals between 1976 and 1978?

8 For which club did Andy Gray play before he joined Wolverhampton Wanderers?

9 Which is the only *English* Football League club to lose in a European Cup Final?

10 Liverpool play at Anfield, but which Scottish club plays at a ground with the same name?

11 Which club had three European Footballers of the Year playing in the forward line at the same time?

12 Liverpool won the League Championship two years in succession in 1976 and 1977. Which was the last team before that to take two consecutive League titles?

31   Away 6

1 With which sport would you associate the terms 'green-some', 'eclectic' and 'Stableford'?

2 This game, said to have begun as a religious ritual among North American Indians, lasted two or three days and was used for training tribal warriors. Introduced to England in 1876, it is now played mainly in the Southeast and Northwest. Its original Indian name was Baggataway but its modern name is French. What is it?

3 Which race has been won in recent years by Lacca Champion, Mutts Silver, Patricia's Hope and Dolores Rocket?

4 In which sport would you find teams competing for the Sugar Bowl, the Orange Bowl, the Cotton Bowl, and the Rose Bowl?

5 Which Englishman won seven World championships in one sport in the fifties, then switched to another sport, and became World Champion in that in 1964?

6 Which was the only discipline in which Nadia Comaneci did *not* get a Gold Medal at the Montreal Olympics?

7 What would you be doing if you went for a strike, but only got a spare?

8 Which woman was British Open Squash champion for sixteen successive years up to 1977?

9 What would you be doing if you were going at 65 miles an hour through Hurricane Alley, Dynamite Corner, Grand Canyon, Times Square, and Broadway?

10 In which sport do you score with a 'spike'?

11 If you are making a Maltese Cross, from a kip, using a planche, where are you?

12 Which sport is said to have been started in the Ootaca-mund Club in Nilgiris, Madras, in the summer of 1875, by Colonel Sir Neville Chamberlain?

32   One-minute Round 7

TEAM A

1 Who was England's youngest-ever Test cricketer?

2 With which sport do you associate the name Sue Brown?

3 Which two boxers were involved in the 'Rumble in the Jungle'?

4 Two marriages between famous Russian sports stars. Can you name the missing husbands?
   a) Irina Rodnina and ......?
   b) Ludmilla Tourischeva and ......?

5 In which countries do these soccer clubs play? a) Independiente, b) Setubal, c) Betis.

TEAM B

1 Who is the only batsman to score six sixes off a six-ball over?

2 Only one post-war Cup Final has been decided outside London. Where was it played?

3 Which two boxers were involved in the 'Thriller in Manila'?

4 The following are two famous sporting fathers and their sporting sons. Can you supply the missing surnames?
   a) Harvey and Robert
   b) Len and Richard

5 In which sports were these people famous? a) Joe di Maggio, b) Louise Brough, c) Paavo Nurmi.

Olympic Champion

Alexander Detiatin won the overall Gold Medal in gymnastics at the 1980 Olympics: in which six disciplines did he have to excel?

33   Home: Soccer 5

1 In the 1982 World Cup Finals in Spain, five countries made their debut. Who were they?

2 Whose was the first £100,000 transfer between British Football League clubs?

3 Who scored the last goal in the 1978 World Cup Final, after Argentina and Holland had had to play extra time?

4 Which player holds the record for the number of appearances in the League?

5 Who is the only man to have both played in and, later, managed his country's World Cup winning side?

6 Who captained Spurs to their League and Cup Double in 1961?

7 The first man to win the European Footballer of the Year award was an Englishman. The year was 1956 – who was the man?

8 The great Pele came out of retirement in 1975 – to play for which club?

9 Which English League club did Argentinian Alex Sabella join in 1978?

10 Which famous First Division manager holds the record for the fastest 200 goals in English soccer?

11 In the 1981 season, two players were leading First Division goal-scorers with 20 goals apiece. Who were they?

12 Billy Wright was well-known as a Wolves player, and as captain of England, but do you know which First Division club he managed between 1962 and 1966?

34   Home: Rugby Union 2

1 In December 1982, Heriot's Former Pupils and Edinburgh Academicals met in a 'Friendly', and wrote them-
selves into the record books. Why?

2 In the 1982 John Player Cup Final, all the points were
scored by two men. Who were they?

3 During the 1981–2 tour of Britain and Ireland, the
Australian team lost twice to club sides. Can you name
them?

4 Who was the French fly-half who proved to be his
country's top points scorer during the 1970s?

5 Who were the last two Englishmen to captain the
British Lions?

6 Who captained the Argentinian team which toured
England in 1978?

7 They held an England XV to a draw in October 1978.
The England team that day contained two men from the
Welsh club, Cardiff. Who were they?

8 Phil Bennett scored 210 points in his international
career. Which player beat that record?

9 In the 1978–9 International Championship season, all
but four of England's points were scored by one man.
Who was he?

10 Which Irishman led the 1955 British Lions on their
historic tour of South Africa, when they prevented the
home country from winning a Test series at home, for
the first time for 27 years?

11 Which is the major trophy for which New Zealand club
sides compete every season?

12 Which player was called out of retirement in 1967 to
captain England against Australia?

35   Home: Darts

1 Who were the Finalists in the 1983 World Professional Championship?

2 The World Masters started in 1974 – who was the first winner?

3 Bobby George won the 1979 News of the World Championship shortly after turning professional. Can you remember whom he defeated in the final?

4 Which player had to withdraw from the 1982 World Professional Championship, when he was stranded in Wales by heavy snow?

5 Who, in 1965, became the first man to retain the *News of the World* title?

6 The 1978 Nations Cup provided a surprise winner. Which was the successful country?

7 Who was the first man to win the World Professional title twice?

8 What is the likeliest way a darts player would throw for a 161 out shot?

9 Which man collected both team and individual titles in the first-ever World Cup, at Wembley in 1977?

10 Who was the first foreign player to win the *News of the World* Championship?

11 Whom did Jocky Wilson defeat in the Final of the 1982 World Professional Championship?

12 When the *News of the World* became a national tournament in 1948, who was the first winner?

Supporters' Club

Here are some visual clues to the nicknames of famous soccer clubs. Can you identify them?

36   Home: Boxing 2

1 In 1979, which boxer did Maurice Hope defeat to win the World Light-middleweight title?

2 Who was the first British boxer to win three Lonsdale Belts outright?

3 Danny McAlinden held the British Heavyweight title for two and a half years in the seventies. Who took it from him?

4 Two Gold Medallists at the Montreal Olympic Games have since become World Professional title holders. Who are they?

5 During the 1970s, three British boxers won World titles in fights abroad. Who are they?

6 In the early sixties, a British boxer and an American boxer fought twice for the World Middleweight title. Who were they?

7 Who was nicknamed 'The Manassa Mauler'?

8 Who is the only boxer to have fought three successive challenges for the World Heavyweight title and to have lost all of them – despite winning the title later?

9 In 1972, Chris Finnegan fought for the World Light-heavyweight title. Who was his opponent?

10 Which British boxer won a Bronze Medal at Light-middleweight at the Munich Olympics, and later became World Champion at a different weight?

11 Joe Brown was World Lightweight Champion between 1959 and 1962. Which British boxer challenged him twice, unsuccessfully, for his title?

12 Who is the only boxer to hold three World titles at the same time?

37   Away 7

1 250,000 schoolchildren and 50,000 adults play this game in Britain alone. It's a seven-a-side game, which allows no physical contact. The first set of official rules was drafted in 1901, from an invention in a YMCA club in America, in 1891. The 1979 World Championships ended in a three-way tie between New Zealand, Australia and Trinidad. What is the game?

2 Who won the women's overall individual title at the World Gymnastics championships in 1978?

3 Born in Hungary, later naturalised a Briton, he won 15 world table tennis titles, and was a major force in the game in the 1930s. Who was he?

4 Imported from France, this pastime of kings was brought to the people by Major John Wingfield. It was his invention 'sphairistike' that was modified by the Marylebone Cricket Club in 1875, to give us the modern game. To this day, the scoring system bears the mark of its more regal days, when a royal clock face was used to record the points. What is it?

5 Which English stadium has staged Test matches in cricket, as well as an FA Cup Final?

6 Which brothers represented England at cricket and rugby union in 1974?

7 Where would you expect to find Knickerbrook?

8 Where does the Oxford and Cambridge Boat Race start and finish?

9 Which British girl became a World Cycling Champion in 1982?

10 Which event was contested for the first time in the 1976 Winter Olympics?

11 In which sport do they refer to the 'York Round'?

12 Apart from athletics, in which two other sports did Britain win Gold Medals in the 1980 Olympic Games?

38   One-minute Round 8

TEAM A

1 With which sport do you associate the name of Maureen Flowers?

2 Which soccer team's home ground is The Den?

3 Two counties shared cricket's four major trophies in 1979. Who were they?

4 In the 1976 Summer Olympic Games, Great Britain won three Gold Medals. Can you name two of the sports involved?

5 Where did these people win Olympic Gold Medals? a) David Hemery, b) Mary Peters, c) Lynn Davies.

TEAM B

1 With which sport do you associate the name of Wendy Norman?

2 Which soccer team's home ground is The Valley?

3 Rugby star Tony O'Reilly was capped 28 times for Ireland. For which two clubs did he play?

4 Britain had three World champions in motor sports in 1976. Can you name two of them?

5 Here are three British Olympic Gold Medallists, but in which event did they win their golds? a) Chris Brasher, in 1956; b) Bob Braithwaite, in 1968; c) Rodney Pattisson, in 1972.

39   Home: Soccer 6

1 Who was the leading goal-scorer in the 1982 World Cup Finals?

2 Jimmy Greaves holds a unique record of having scored on his debut for every club for which he has played. Can you name his clubs?

3 Who were the first winners of the World Cup in 1930?

4 In 1979, which two Scottish sides had 29 postponements in their attempt to play a Scottish FA Cup Tie?

5 Ajax had a hat-trick of European Cup wins in 1971–2–3. Which teams did they defeat in those Finals?

6 Who were the last pair of brothers to play in an FA Cup Final?

7 Only three players have scored hat-tricks in the European Cup Final. Who are they?

8 In the 1960s, a pair of brothers were capped for two different countries – one for England, one for Wales. Who were they?

9 The UEFA Cup was previously called the Fairs Cup. Which club, in 1968, became the first British team to win the trophy?

10 For the next five years, English clubs won the UEFA Cup. Who finally stopped our winning streak, beating Spurs in the 1974 final?

11 Which was the first British team to win the European Cup-Winners' Cup?

12 Which Football League club is known by the nickname 'The Pilgrims'?

40   Home: Cricket 3

1 Jim Laker's Test match record of 19 wickets against Australia is well-known, but on which ground did he achieve the feat?

2 In the 1974 England v Pakistan Test series, only 3 centuries were scored – all in the Third Test at the Oval. Can you name the century-makers?

3 England won the Ashes in 1953. Who was their captain?

4 Who were the first winners of the Gillette (now Nat-West) Cup?

5 A famous English bowler took over 200 wickets in both the 1955 and 1957 seasons. Who was he?

6 Hobbs and Sutcliffe are always mentioned in the same breath, but Hobbs did open the batting with another famous Yorkshireman, and together they broke the record for a first-wicket partnership against Australia. Who was the other man?

7 The Benson and Hedges Cup was introduced in 1972. Who were the first winners?

8 In 1925, Jack Hobbs scored 16 centuries in a season. Who eventually broke that record?

9 Clive Lloyd was preceded, as West Indies captain, by another player from Guyana, as he is. Who was that player?

10 Derbyshire reached the Final of the Gillette Cup in 1969, for the first time, but were beaten. Who defeated them?

11 Wicket-keeper Godfrey Evans had a record 219 dismissals in Test Matches. Who broke that record in the 1971–2 winter season?

12 Who has captained the England Test team the greatest number of times?

Which County?

Which County cricket teams wear these badges?

a

b   INVICTA

c

d

e

f

g

41   Home: Athletics 4

1 The British record for the Women's 1500-Metres stood for seven years, from 1972 to 1979. Who set it in 1972?

2 Who eventually broke this record in 1979?

3 In the 1978 Commonwealth Games, a Welshman won the Men's 110-Metres Hurdles. Who was he?

4 Who was the first pole-vaulter to clear 19 feet?

5 Two athletes have retained the Olympic 10,000-Metre title. Who are they?

6 Which English girl won the Gold in the 400-Metres in the Commonwealth Games in Edmonton?

7 In August 1980, the marvellous East German Ladies' Squad set World Relay records at 100-Metres and 200-Metres in the space of nine days. Three girls ran in both races. Who were they?

8 In the 1970 Commonwealth Games, an English husband and wife won Gold Medals on the same day. Who were they?

9 Who is the only woman athlete to win a medal in four successive Olympic Games?

10 An Australian girl won the hurdles at three successive Commonwealth Games – in 1962, 1966 and 1970. Who was she?

11 Since the war, only two men have done the sprint double at the Olympics. Who are they?

12 Which two famous athletes acted as pacemakers for Roger Bannister when he ran the first four-minute mile?

The gateways to two famous sporting venues.
Where are they?

Who are they?

3

4

5

6

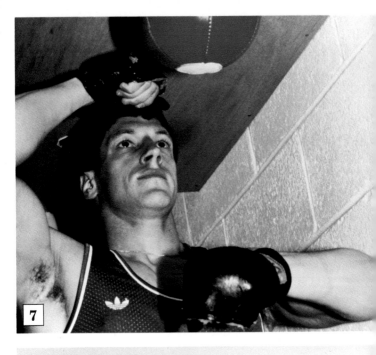

7

8

11

12

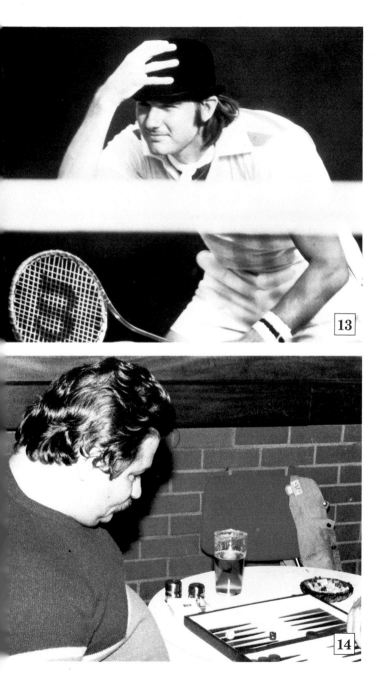

Can you identify these two famous sports grounds?

I bring you a Message . . .

The modern Pentathlon is based on the story of a king's messenger facing and conquering dangers to deliver a message for his master. In which five sports does the modern Pentathlete have to excel?

42 Home: Tennis 2

1 Who is the youngest player to win the US Open Ladies' Singles?

2 Which Australian reached the Final of the Men's Singles at Wimbledon three years in succession during the 1960s, and each time was beaten?

3 Louise Brough won the Wimbledon Women's Doubles title five times, the French doubles three times, and the US Doubles 13 times – a remarkable record, and all with the same partner. Who was she?

4 Rod Laver won the Wimbledon Men's Singles four times, but he was also defeated twice in the Final – by whom?

5 In 1960, a British pair were the losing finalists in the Wimbledon Men's Doubles. Who were they?

6 Martina Navratilova is Czech-born, but who was the last Czech woman to appear in a Wimbledon Singles Final before her?

7 Only two women have achieved the Grand Slam – who were they?

8 Russia's first appearance in a Wimbledon Final came in 1968, in the Mixed Doubles. Who were the players?

9 In 1983, America, the holders of the Davis Cup were unexpectedly beaten in the first round of their defence of it. By which country?

10 Since the war, three all-Australian combinations have won the Women's Doubles at Wimbledon. Can you name them?

11 Who is the only unseeded player to reach the Wimbledon Men's Singles Final *twice*?

12 Althea Gibson won the Wimbledon Women's Doubles three years in succession, with three different partners – one British, one American, one South American. Who were they?

Wimbledon Finalist

The popular Ken Rosewall never won the Wimbledon Men's Singles, but he did reach the Final four times. Who defeated him?

43   One-minute Round 9

TEAM A

1 Where is the Maracana Stadium?

2 Which is the only throwing event in athletics confined to men?

3 During 1971, three British boxers held the European Heavyweight title. Can you name two of them?

4 Which British horse and rider won an individual Silver Medal in Show Jumping, at the 1968 Olympics in Mexico?

5 Can you fill in the missing names on this list of Wimbledon Women's Singles Champions? 1973 King, 1974 ......? 1975 King, 1976 Evert, 1977 ......?, 1978 ......?, 1979 Navratilova.

TEAM B

1 Where is Ellis Park?

2 In which athletics event did Paul Nihill break a World record in 1972?

3 Only two English soccer clubs have appeared in the Final of all three major European competitions. Can you name them?

4 Which horse and rider won an individual Bronze Medal in the Show Jumping at the 1968 Olympics in Mexico?

5 Can you fill in the missing names in this list of World Champion Drivers? 1973 Jackie Stewart, 1974............?, 1975 Niki Lauda, 1976 ....?, 1977 Niki Lauda, 1978.........?, 1979 Jody Scheckter.

44   Home: Horse Racing 3

1 Where is the Great Northern Derby held?

2 Pat Taaffe had two Grand National victories. Which horses did he ride?

3 Pat Taaffe also rode two *different* horses to victory in the Cheltenham Gold Cup. Can you name them?

4 Which horse sired the great French filly Dahlia?

5 Which was the only horse ever to beat Brigadier Gerard?

6 Who was the last jockey to win both the Champion Hurdle and the Cheltenham Gold Cup in the same season?

7 The great Ribot has sired four St Leger winners. Can you name them?

8 Can you name the American-bred horse, trained by Vincent O'Brien, and ridden by Lester Piggott, which won the *Prix de l'Arc de Triomphe* in 1978, for the second year running?

9 Who was the last Flat Race champion jockey to win the title with more than 200 winners?

10 Which three races comprise the American Triple Crown?

11 Monksfield won the Champion Hurdle in 1978 and 1979. Can you name the jockeys who rode him?

12 Steve Cauthen's first classic winner in England came on only his second mount in an English classic. Can you name the horse?

45   Home: Rugby League

1 The 1982 Challenge Cup Final ended in a 14–14 draw. Which two clubs were involved?

2 Mick Parrish went through two seasons scoring in every game for two different clubs – the only player to achieve this feat. Which were the two clubs?

3 One player went through two seasons scoring in every game, but with the same club. Can you name the player and the club?

4 Which player missed a last-minute conversion, which would have given his side the Rugby League Challenge Cup in 1968?

5 Jim Sullivan of Wigan had a career record of 6,192 points. Who took that record from him?

6 Who was the first player to be sent off in a Challenge Cup Final at Wembley?

7 David Watkins scored 493 points in a season, just 3 short of the all-time record. By whom was this record held?

8 Which side clinched their first championship title for 76 years in 1982?

9 Bradford Northern appeared at Wembley for the Challenge Cup Final for three years running – in 1947, 1948 and 1949. It was some time before this feat was achieved again – by which team?

10 The Lance Todd Trophy is awarded to the Man of the Match in the Challenge Cup Final: of which club was Lance Todd the manager?

11 Which player captained his club in six Challenge Cup Finals between 1958 and 1966?

12 Which club won all their 26 League matches in the 1978–9 season?

Olympic Teams

Seven team games were included in the 1980 Olympic Games. Can you name them?

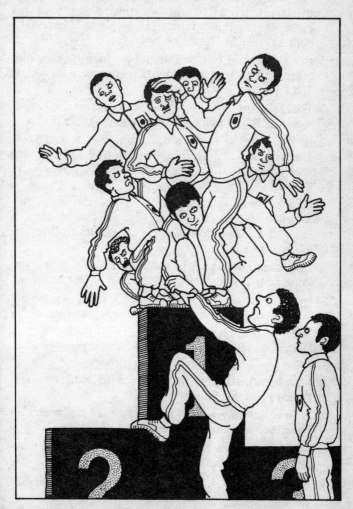

46   Home: Golf 2

1 On the 17th hole of this course there stands a plaque commemorating a magnificent shot by Bobby Jones, the last American to win the British Open there. Six championships have been held there since. Where is the course?

2 Royal Birkdale boasts a similar plaque to commemorate a miraculous shot by another American golfer. Who was he?

3 Tom Watson, in the first of his British Open victories, was involved in a play-off. Who was the other player?

4 In 1979, the Ryder Cup rules were changed to allow Europeans to play alongside British Isles players. That year, only two Europeans were selected. Who were they?

5 Hubert Green won the 1977 US Open, despite a hoax telephone call threatening his life as he played. He also beat off a tremendous last-minute challenge from the 1975 US Open champion. Who was that?

6 Ben Hogan won the British and American Opens in the same year, 1953. Who was the next golfer to do the same?

7 Who was the first foreigner after the war to win the US Open?

8 Who was captain of the last Ryder Cup team to beat the United States outright?

9 Only two Australians have won the British Open. Who are they?

10 Who is the only man to have won the US and British Open *and* Amateur titles in the same year?

11 Bob Charles won the 1963 British Open after a play-off – against whom?

12 Who was the first American golfer to win the British Open?

47   Home: Three-day Eventing

1 In the last twenty years, only two non-British riders have won Badminton. Who are they?

2 An American rider, on a horse called Irish Cap, won the World Individual Championship at Burghley in 1974. Who was he?

3 The horses Great Ovation, Columbus, and Lincoln all won Badminton – with which rider?

4 Who were the first winners of the World Team Championship in 1966?

5 In the 1971 European Championships, Great Britain swept the board, winning the team and all the individual medals. Who were the individual medallists?

6 Who was the first woman to win the World Championship, and on which horse?

7 Who were Richard Meade's team-mates with whom he won the Team Gold Medal at the Mexico Olympic Games?

8 Which horse and rider won the European Championship in 1955, Badminton, an Olympic Individual Bronze and a Team Gold Medal in 1956?

9 In the 1973 European Championships at Kiev, which girl, despite a dreadful fall, carried on, hoping to give the British team a medal?

10 Which horse and rider won the Individual Gold Medal at the Munich Olympics?

11 Who was in the British team which won the Team Gold at the Munich Olympics?

12 Which rider scored a hat-trick of Badminton victories on the horses High and Mighty and Airs and Graces?

48　One-minute Round 10

TEAM A

1 In which sport is Desmond Douglas a famous name?

2 Who was John McEnroe's partner in his 1981 and 1983 Wimbledon Men's Doubles victories?

3 There are three field events in which women athletes do not compete. One is the hammer, what are the other two?

4 Which are the two trophies (men's and women's) competed for in badminton, between teams from different countries?

5 Can you supply the first names of these famous sporting Rowes? a) .... Rowe (shot put), b) .... Rowe (table tennis), c) .... Rowe (cricket).

TEAM B

1 In which sport is Mike Hazelwood a famous name?

2 Which British speedway rider won the World title in 1980?

3 Which two clubs were involved in the first all-London FA Cup Final?

4 Which are the two trophies (men's and women's) competed for in table tennis between teams from different countries?

5 Can you fill in the first names of these famous sporting Joneses? a) .... Jones (motor racing), b) .... Jones (tennis), c) .... Jones (golf).

Playing Away

Denis Law was one of Scotland's greatest footballers: which four clubs did he play for during his career?

49 Home: Soccer 7

1 In the 1970s, three footballers played in two FA Cup Finals at Wembley with different clubs. Who are they?

2 The oldest man to appear in an international match for Wales, was also one of the few men to spend his entire football career with two clubs in the same city – Manchester. Who was he?

3 Only two managers have taken two different clubs to the First Division title. Who are they?

4 With which famous Hungarian club side did the great star Ferenc Puskas make his name?

5 Former England manager Ron Greenwood played for four clubs. Can you name two of them?

6 Despite always providing formidable teams, the USSR has only once reached the Semi-finals of the World Cup. When was that?

7 Leeds United have been on the losing side three times in Wembley FA Cup Finals since the war. Can you name the three sides who have beaten them?

8 In 1967, two famous goalkeepers were involved in a freakish incident, where one sent a long kick down the pitch, and scored in his opponent's net. Who were the two goalkeepers?

9 Arsenal did the League and Cup Double in 1971. Which was the last club to do the Double before that?

10 Which Football League club is known by the nickname 'The Millers'?

11 Real Madrid won the European Cup for the first five years of its existence. Which team took the trophy after them, and then beat them in the Final the following year?

12 Which famous player captained England in the 1962 World Cup Finals?

50　Home: Athletics 5

1　Since the war, two women have won Golds in both the Olympic 200-Metres and the 400-Metres (not in the same year). Who are they?

2　In the 1978 Commonwealth Games, Brendan Foster was beaten into third place in the 5000-Metres by two Kenyans. Who were they?

3　Which woman, in June 1980, broke the World record for the 100-Metres Hurdles?

4　Can you name the male javelin thrower who has won four European Gold Medals, and Olympic Gold, Silver and Bronze? In fact, he failed by just one inch, in Munich, to retain the Gold he won in Mexico.

5　Tatiana Kazankina won the 800-Metres in the Montreal Olympics in a World record time. A month earlier she had set a World record over another distance. What was it?

6　Who was the first athlete to win two Gold Medals in the Olympic Decathlon?

7　Who was the only British girl to reach an individual track Final at the 1976 Olympic Games?

8　Who won the Gold Medal in the Men's Pole Vault at the Moscow Olympics?

9　Australian girls did the double in the sprints at both the 1952 and 1956 Olympic Games. Who were the two athletes?

10　Only one athlete has won four consecutive Gold Medals in the Olympics in the same event. Who is he?

11　Who held the Men's Long Jump World record before Bob Beamon's mighty leap at the Mexico Olympics?

12　Who was the first man to put the shot over 70 feet?

51   Home: Judo

1 Which girl won six British titles in the 1970s – five Heavyweight and one Open?

2 In which Olympic Games was judo first introduced?

3 Which judo player won four World Middleweight titles in the 1970s?

4 Two new weight divisions were introduced to the judo events in the 1972 Olympics. Can you name them?

5 Who was the first non-Japanese judo player to win a World title?

6 Which two British judo players won Bronze Medals in the 1972 Olympic Games?

7 Which British judo player won a Silver Medal in the Open category at the Montreal Olympics?

8 The same man also competed in the Heavyweight class at those Games, and was beaten by the eventual Gold Medallist. Who was he?

9 Who was the first Briton to win a World judo title?

10 Who was the Dutch judo player who won Gold Medals in both the Open and Heavyweight categories at the 1972 Olympic Games?

11 An English girl won a Gold Medal in the Under-48 Kilos class in the first-ever Ladies World Championships in 1980. Who was she?

12 1982 saw a British girl win both World and European Championship titles in the Under-48 Kilos class. Who was she?

52   Home: Boxing 3

1 From which British boxer did Matteo Salvemini take the European Middleweight title in October 1980?

2 Two months later, Salvemini lost the title to another British boxer. Who was he?

3 Which brothers both won Gold Medals in boxing in the 1976 Olympics?

4 Which Cornish boxer was British and Empire champion at Heavyweight, Light-heavyweight and Middleweight?

5 And which Cornish-born boxer was *World* champion at Heavyweight, Light-heavyweight and Middleweight – the first fighter to win three World titles?

6 Who took the World Lightweight crown from Ken Buchanan in 1972?

7 Who won the Middleweight Gold Medal at the 1982 Commonwealth Games?

8 Who did Joe Louis beat in 1937, to become World Heavyweight Champion for the first time?

9 In 1981, who took the World Light-middleweight title from Maurice Hope?

10 Only one World Heavyweight Champion was undefeated throughout his career. Who was he?

11 Which boxer achieved his third successive Gold Medal at the Moscow Olympics?

12 Dick Richardson won the European Heavyweight Championship in 1960. Who took the title from him two years later?

53   Away 8

1 Which Russian woman gymnast has won eighteen Olympic medals – more than any other person, in any other sport?

2 Who, or what, is Watkins Glen?

3 Which British cyclist won the world 5000-Metres Pursuit title in 1970?

4 In which sport did Vladimir Alexeyev win Gold Medals at the Munich and Montreal Olympics?

5 Who competes for the Eisenhower Trophy?

6 Britain won two Silver Medals in rowing at the 1976 Olympics. In which events?

7 Which sport was first played in the Olympics in Berlin in 1936, but not re-introduced until 1972?

8 Which sport mainly takes place between 5 and 1 – but generally finishes between 7 and 8?

9 During the Second World War, the Royal Automobile Club took over the administration of this sport, which derives from an older game played at Harrow School. The British version is played world-wide, except in America, where the scoring is different. Only in the women's game do the two codes compete, that being when they play for the Wolfe-Noel Cup. What is the sport?

10 Who was the first man to win three TT events in one year?

11 Clive van Ryneveld's sporting career was unusual – in what way?

12 This woman retired from athletics at the age of eighteen, with two Olympic Gold Medals. She went on to become the world's leading woman golfer, and she wasn't bad at baseball and tennis either! Who was she?

Decathlon Champion

Daley Thompson is the World Champion Decathlete. In which ten events must he compete?

54   One-minute Round 11

TEAM A

1 Where is Powderhall?

2 In which sport is Klaus Dibiasi a former champion?

3 Two speedway riders have each won the World Championship a record five times. Can you name them?

4 Two British athletes have won Olympic Gold Medals since the war in race walking. Who are they?

5 In which countries would you find these sporting venues? a) Sabina Park, b) Bernabeu, c) Dundrod.

TEAM B

1 Where is the King George VI and Queen Elizabeth Stakes run?

2 In which sport was Hashim Khan a star?

3 Which two countries play for the FM Worrell Trophy?

4 Which two Czechoslovak-born players have won the Men's Singles at Wimbledon since the war?

5 At which sporting venues would you find these names? a) Dingle Dell, b) Quarter Bridge, c) Vauxhall End.

55   Home: Soccer 8

1 Which is the oldest existing club in the Football League?

2 Who, in 1970, became the first player to be transferred, between British clubs, for £200,000?

3 Who beat Liverpool in the 1981 World Club Championship?

4 Who was the last player to score more than 50 goals in a Football League season?

5 West Germany have appeared in four World Cup Finals, but whom did they beat in their first Final in 1954?

6 Since the war, only two clubs have won the FA Cup two years in succession. Which clubs are they?

7 The European Cup started in 1955: which was the first English club to compete in it?

8 Which Football League club is known by the nickname The Cobblers?

9 When Stanley Matthews retired as a player, of which club did he become manager?

10 Gordon Banks was ever-present in the England goal in the 1966 World Cup Finals, preventing the appearance of the two other goalkeepers in the squad. Who were they?

11 Only one player has ever scored a hat-trick in an FA Cup Final at Wembley. Who was that?

12 Who captained the West German side which played England in the 1966 World Cup Final?

56   Home: Badminton

1 Which family collected sixteen All-England Badminton titles between 1925 and 1967?

2 Who is the only Swedish woman since the war to win the All-England Badminton Singles?

3 In the 1983 World Championships, Norah Perry won the Mixed Doubles title. Who was her partner?

4 Liem-Swie King won the All-England Men's Singles two years running – in 1978 and 1979. Can you name the men he defeated in those Finals?

5 Which man made a hundred appearances for the England team between 1951 and 1970?

6 In the 1983 World Championships, the reigning Women's Doubles champions were defeated in the final. Who were they?

7 Only one woman successfully retained the All-England badminton Singles title during the 1970s. Who was she?

8 Who, in the 1970 Commonwealth Games, won a Gold Medal for Canada?

9 Which British girl won a Bronze Medal at the 1983 World Championships?

10 Which British pair won the European Men's Doubles in 1976 and 1978?

11 In 1924, one woman won both the All-England Badminton Singles, and the Wimbledon tennis Singles. Who was she?

12 In the Ladies' Singles at the 1970 Commonwealth Games, Great Britain swept the board, winning all three medals. Who were the medallists?

Doubles Partners

Billie-Jean King has won the Wimbledon Women's Doubles ten times, with five different partners. Can you name them?

1 The 1982 Welsh Challenge Cup Final ended in a 12–12 draw, but Cardiff took the Cup. Why?

2 England won the International Championship in 1980, under Bill Beaumont's captaincy. Who was the last English captain before him to achieve that feat?

3 Who would you expect to find at Raeburn Place?

4 Which Welsh international won an Olympic Silver Medal in the sprint relay in the 1948 Olympics?

5 What was unique about the Five Nations' Championship of 1973?

6 In 1910, Jack Bancroft scored a record 19 points for Wales against France. In 1967, another Welshman equalled that points tally. Who was he?

7 Which three players made up the famous Pontypool front row?

8 Which international player rejoiced in the nickname 'Pinetree'?

9 Which Welsh club had a run of seventy home matches without defeat in the mid-sixties?

10 In which country do provincial rugby sides compete for the Carling Bowl?

11 The French won the International Championship outright for the first time in the 1958–9 season. Who was their captain?

12 Andy Hancock is renowned for his brilliant try against Scotland, but in fact he only gained two more caps altogether, both against the same country. Which one?

58 Home: Athletics 6

1 When were the Olympic Games last staged in Great Britain?

2 Who was the first woman to win an Olympic Gold Medal in the Pentathlon?

3 The Women's 100-Metres Hurdles Gold Medal, in both the 1974 and 1978 Commonwealth Games, went to English women. Who were they?

4 Which British athlete won the women's 400-Metres in the European Indoor Championships three times in the 1970s?

5 Twelve medals – nine Gold, and three Silver – were won by one man in the three Olympic Games in the 1920s. Who was he?

6 In the 1978 Commonwealth Games, which country took a surprise Gold Medal in the Men's 4 × 100-Metres Relay?

7 Which man won both the 5000-Metres and 10,000-Metres in the 1956 Olympic Games?

8 Who won Britain's only Gold Medal in the 1978 European Championships?

9 Which Australian girl won the 800-Metres in the 1978 Commonwealth Games?

10 Who was the first woman sprinter to defend successfully an Olympic title?

11 Which woman won the 1500-Metres in both the Moscow and Montreal Olympics?

12 Who is the only man to have won two Olympic Gold Medals in the 400-Metres Hurdles?

59   Home: Horse Racing 4

1 Which was the first horse to win the King George VI and Queen Elizabeth Stakes twice?

2 Which man trained four Grand National winners between 1956 and 1976?

3 In his long career as a jockey, Sir Gordon Richards rode only one Derby winner. What was the name of the horse?

4 On which two different horses did Brian Fletcher win the Grand National?

5 What do 'Persian War', 'Sir Ken' and 'Hatton's Grace' have in common?

6 Who, in 1955, became the first man to train three Grand National winners in successive years?

7 In 1977, Willie Carson won both the Oaks and the St Leger on the same horse. Can you name the horse?

8 Who was the first woman to ride in the Grand National?

9 Who was the first woman to complete the Grand National?

10 The November Handicap is now run at Doncaster, but where was its original venue?

11 Everyone knows the story of how Devon Loch unaccountably fell in the 1956 Grand National, but who was his jockey?

12 Which American horse established a new World winnings record in 1982?

Seven Events

Judy Livermore is Britain's leading competitor in a comparatively new event – the heptathlon. What are the seven events involved?

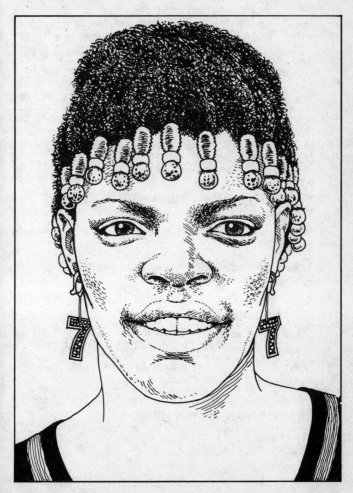

1 When Alex Higgins won the World Championship in 1982, he was taken to the Final and deciding frame in two matches. Can you name the men he so narrowly defeated?

2 Which country won the State Express World Team Classic for the first two years of the competition?

3 The late – and great – Joe Davis won the World Professional Snooker title every year from its inception in 1927, to his retirement in 1946. Who succeeded him in 1947 as World Champion?

4 Who is the only non-British player to have won the World Professional Championship?

5 Dennis Taylor and Alex Higgins were in the 1981 Northern Ireland team for the State Express World Team Classic. Who was the third member of the team?

6 Who were the beaten Semi-finalists in the 1983 World Professional Championship?

7 Who won the first United Kingdom Professional title in 1977?

8 How many balls do you have to pot to achieve the maximum 147 break?

9 Who was the first man to win the World Amateur Championship twice?

10 Who were the last two overseas players to reach the Final of the World Professional Championship?

11 Who is the youngest player to have won the World Professional title?

12 Which player currently holds the World record for the highest number of maximum breaks?

61   One-minute Round 12

TEAM A

1 With which sport do you associate the name Rudy Hartono?

2 At which cricket ground would you find the Radcliffe Road end?

3 In 1959, the Wimbledon Singles titles were both won by South Americans. Who were they?

4 Can you name the skaters who won the Men's and Women's Figure Skating titles at the 1976 Winter Olympics?

5 Can you fill in the missing names in this list of FA Cup-winning managers? 1972: Don Revie, 1973: ......?, 1974: Bill Shankly, 1975: ......?, 1976: Lawrie McMenemy, 1977: ......?, 1978: Bobby Robson.

TEAM B

1 With which sport do you associate Bisley?

2 Which cricketer has the middle name Dylan?

3 Which two cyclists have each won the *Tour de France* a record five times?

4 Brazil won the Soccer World Cup three times. Can you name two of the teams they defeated in the Final?

5 Can you fill in the missing names in this list of Commonwealth Games venues? 1958: Cardiff, 1962: ......?, 1966: Kingston, Jamaica, 1970: ......?, 1974: ......?, 1978: Edmonton.

Answers

1   One-minute Round 1

TEAM A

1 Royal Birkdale.
2 Guy and Lillian Camberabero.
3 Bobby-Joe Morrow: athletics (double sprint Gold Medallist 1956 Olympics); Jeanette Altweg: ice-skating (1951–2 World Champion).
4 Allan Wells and Mike McFarlane.
5 1982 – West Germany; 1978 – Holland; 1974 – Holland.

TEAM B

1 Brisbane (Australia).
2 USSR (in 1956, 1964, 1972, 1980).
3 Ford (ice-dancing); Nash (bobsleigh).
4 Dick Saunders on Grittar.
5 a) Billie Jean King; b) Margaret Court; c) Mariana Borg.

2   Home: Soccer 1

1 Pele (Brazil: 1958 and 1970); Vava (Brazil: 1958 and 1962); Breitner (W. Germany: 1974 and 1982).
2 Kenny Dalglish; Sir Stanley Matthews; Tom Finney; Danny Blanchflower.
3 Steve Heighway (1971 and 1974).
4 Bobby Smith.
5 Dennis Mortimer.
6 Gordon McQueen and Sammy McIlroy (Manchester United); Alan Sunderland (Arsenal).
7 Tommy Gemmell.
8 Steve Daley, Kevin Reeves and Trevor Francis.
9 Borussia Munchengladbach.

10 Manchester United (v Benfica in 1968); Leeds United (v Bayern Munich 1975).
11 Malcolm Macdonald.
12 Tottenham Hotspurs.

Which Club?

a) Liverpool; b) Manchester United; c) Cardiff City; d) Preston North End; e) Southampton; f) Ipswich Town.

3   Home: Athletics 1

1 Peter Snell (New Zealand; 1964).
2 Brendan Foster (Bronze, 10,000-Metres).
3 Raelene Boyle.
4 Denise Boyd.
5 Bob Seagren (USA).
6 Wolfgang Nordwig (GDR).
7 Tommy Smith (USA).
8 Ann Packer (1964); Lillian Board (1968).
9 Nikolai Avilov (1972).
10 Dana Zatopek.
11 Alan Pascoe.
12 She was the first woman to run a mile in under five minutes.

4   Home: Horse Racing 1

1 Gianfranco Dettori (of Italy).
2 Doncaster (the Lincoln course is closed).
3 Nagwa.
4 Alexandra Park.
5 Ile de Bourbon (1978).
6 Never Say Die.
7 Meriel Tufnell.
8 Vulgan.

94

9 Josh Gifford on Rosyth.
10 Tulyar.
11 The Oaks and the 1,000-Guineas.
12 Arkle (1964–5–6).

5 Away 1

1 Basketball.
2 The world's largest golf bunker – on the Pine Valley course, New Jersey, USA.
3 Speedway.
4 Gina Swift.
5 On the Cresta Run.
6 She became the first paraplegic to win a Gold Medal (in Ladies' Archery).
7 Whitbread Village Cricket Final.
8 Billiards: (the term is used when each player strikes the white from the baulk line, up the table, and back. The ball finishing nearest the baulk line 'wins', and that player decides whether he wants to break, or put his opponent 'in').
9 Ann Jones (then Ann Haydon), Wimbledon champion in 1969.
10 Football and cricket.
11 Shooting (an international match between teams from different countries).
12 MCC – they were the founder members, in 1787, of the Marylebone Cricket Club.

Who's This?

a) Sebastian Coe; b) Trevor Brooking; c) Willie Carson; d) Charlie Nicholas; e) Steve Cram; f) Lucinda Green; g) Steve Davis.

6   One-minute Round 2

1 France.
2 David Broome.
3 Alex Higgins and Ray Reardon.
4 Roger Bannister and John Landy.
5 a) Adrian Moorhouse; b) Andy Astbury; c) Phil Hubble.

TEAM B

1 Leeds United.
2 Dennis Sigalos.
3 Vault; asymetric bars.
4 Dave Starbrook: judo.
5 a) Geoff Lewis; b) Pat Eddery; c) Willie Carson.

Wimbledon Winners

Borg defeated: 1976, Nastase; 1977 and 1988, Connors; 1979, Tanner; 1980, McEnroe.
He was beaten by: 1973, Roger Taylor (Quarter-Final); 1974, Ismael El-Shafei (Round 3); 1975, Arthur Ashe (Quarter-Final); 1981, John McEnroe (Final).

7   Home: Cricket 1

1 Keith Boyce (Barbados and Essex).
2 Geoffrey Boycott (*1st and 2nd*); Brian Luckhurst (*3rd and 4th*); Barry Wood (*5th*).
3 Bob Massie (Australia; 16 for 137 at Lords in 1972).
4 West Indies beat Australia by 17 runs.
5 England (beaten by Australia); New Zealand (beaten by West Indies).
6. Sheffield.
7 Mushtaq Mohammed of Pakistan.
8 Graham Gooch.
9 Durham (beat Yorkshire in 1973).

10 John Reid.
11 Kent (1973, 1976 and 1978).
12 It was the first *women's* Test to be played at Lords.

8   Home: Swimming and Diving

1 Chris Snode.
2 Dawn Fraser (100-Metres Freestyle, 1956, 60 and 64).
3 Brian Phelps.
4 The Butterfly Stroke.
5 Shirley Babashoff.
6 Rome (1960) in the 200-Metres Breast Stroke.
7 Klaus Dibiasi (1968, 72 and 76).
8 John Hencken (Gold 1972, Silver 1976); David Wilkie (Silver 1972, Gold 1976).
9 Liz Ferris (Bronze, 1960).
10 Debbie Meyer.
11 Judy Grinham.
12 Roland Matthes (100-Metres and 200-Metres).

9   Home: Boxing 1

1 John H. Stracey.
2 Jose Napoles.
3 Bombadier Billy Wells, in 1916.
4 Floyd Patterson (Middleweight Gold 1952; World title 1956).
5 Howard Winstone.
6 Richard Dunne.
7 Kevin Finnegan.
8 Dave Boy Green.
9 Roberto Duran of Panama.
10 Rodrigo Valdes.
11 Sonny Liston (1964); George Foreman (1974); Leon Spinks (1978).
12 Sugar Ray Robinson (Middleweight).

Six times Three

Anneli Drummond-Hay; Richard Meade; Sheila Willcox (now Waddington); Mark Phillips; Jane Holderness-Roddam; Lucinda Prior-Palmer (now Green).

10   Away 2

1 Basketball.
2 Bobbi is a woman – the first in fifty years to race against men on a speedway track in this country, in an international indoor championship.
3 Rugby Union – it's competed for at the Middlesex Sevens.
4 Beth Heiden.
5 Hockey.
6 Thorpe Park.
7 Polo.
8 They are ice-dance routines.
9 Black: graded belts in judo.
10 Jim Fox, Adrian Parker and Danny Nightingale.
11 Golf (holes 9, 4, and 8 respectively on the US Masters Course, Augusta, Georgia).
12 Squash.

11   One-minute Round 3

TEAM A

1 David Hemery, in 1968.
2 United States.
3 a) Athletics – West Germany; b) Tennis – Czechoslovakia.
4 Wimbledon (1977); Wigan (1978).
5 a) Hugh Porter, b) David Mould, c) Robbie Brightwell.

TEAM B

1 Chelsea.
2 The St Leger.
3 a) 1500-Metres, b) Hammer.
4 a) Gullikson, b) Mayer.
5 a) Hoylake, b) Royal Lytham and St Annes, c) Sandwich.

12   Home: Soccer 2

1 Kevin Keegan (Liverpool, 1974); Alan Taylor (West Ham, 1975).
2 Phil Thompson.
3 Leicester City (1965–74); Stoke City (1974–7); Nottingham Forest (1977–82).
4 Ipswich.
5 Aston Villa and Everton. (Villa eventually won.)
6 Hillsborough (Sheffield Wednesday); Old Trafford (Manchester United).
7 Steve Archibald (Aberdeen to Spurs for £800,000 in May 1980).
8 Keith Burkinshaw (Spurs 1981 and 1982); John Lyall (West Ham 1975 and 1980).
9 Arsenal, beaten by Valencia of Spain.
10 David Fairclough.
11 Mario Kempes (6 goals).
12 Billy Bremner (for Leeds United).

13   Home: Tennis 1

1 Czechoslovakia (Ivan Lendl and Hana Mandlikova).
2 Ross Case and Geoff Masters.
3 John Newcombe (in 1970).
4 Evonne Cawley (née Goolagong) in 1972 and 1975.
5 Rod Laver (1962 and 1969).
6 Angela Mortimer (in 1961).
7 Owen Davidson (1967, 1971, 1973, and 1974).
8 Anne Hobbs, Michele Tyler, Sue Mappin.
9 Darlene Hard (1959); Sandra Reynolds (1960); Margaret Smith (1964).
10 Wilhelm Bungert.
11 Shirley Fry.
12 Angela Mortimer and Anne Shilcock.

14   Home: Motor Racing

1 Belgian.
2 Phil Hill (1961).
3 Jackie Stewart (1971 and 1973); James Hunt (1976).
4 Nurburgring.
5 Jacky Ickx of Belgium.
6 Giuseppe Farina.
7 East London.
8 Graham Hill.
9 Denny Hulme (1967).
10 Phil Hill and Olivier Gendebien.
11 Silverstone, Brands Hatch and Aintree.
12 Swiss.

Speedway Special

1976: John Louis; 1977: Peter Collins; 1978: Gordon Kennett.

15   Away 3

1 Lake Placid (1932 and 1980); Squaw Valley (1960).
2 Yachting.
3 Ice-skating: they are compulsory figures.
4 Archery (arrows and distances for the Men's Double FITA).
5 Wimbledon Lawn Tennis Championships.
6 Tennis.
7 Zimbabwe for Ladies' hockey.
8 Trampolining.
9 Cycling: it is the twelfth stage of the Tour de France – 153 miles over cobbles.
10 Crosby (Bing, Kathy, Mary, Nathaniel).
11 Canoeing (a 360° turn in a kayak).
12 You have to be called Bobby Jones to play in it. (Entry only upon production of birth certificate).

16   One-minute Round 4

TEAM A

1 Pam Shriver.
2 The Crucible Theatre, Sheffield.
3 The Hill: Sydney Cricket Ground; The Chair: Aintree Grand National Course.
4 Kent and Middlesex (1977).
5 a) ice-skating, b) snooker and billiards, c) gymnastics – a type of vault.

TEAM B

1 Augusta, Georgia.
2 Rotterdam.
3 a) Argentina, b) USA.
4 Heather Hunt (now Oakes); Kathy Smallwood (now Cook); Bev Goddard (now Callender); Sonia Lannaman.
5 a) Emlyn Hughes, b) Eric Bristow, c) Alberto Juantorena.

17   Home: Athletics 2

1 Amos Biwott (Gold); Ben Kogo (Silver).
2 Kip Keino (Gold); Ben Jipcho (Silver).
3 Dave Bedford.
4 Sheila Lerwill (1952); Thelma Hopkins (1956); Dorothy Shirley (1960).
5 Ludmilla Bragina of USSR.
6 Ann Packer (800-Metres, 1964).
7 Ralph Boston.
8 Tokyo, in 1964.
9 Mike Bull of Northern Ireland.
10 Dave Moorcroft (Gold 1500-Metres Commonwealth; Bronze 1500-Metres European).
11 Livio Berutti (1960); Pietro Mennea (1980).
12 Gordon Pirie (Silver 1956); Derek Ibbotson (Bronze 1956); Ian Stewart (Bronze 1972).

Backwards to Victory

Rowing; tug-of-war; backstroke.

18   Home: Rugby Union 1

1 The same fifteen men played in all four matches; they didn't concede a try during the championship.
2 The British Lions (normally a touring side).
3 Willie Duggan.
4 Ian McLauchlan.
5 Jacques Fouroux.
6 Ray Gravell and J. J. Williams.
7 Nigel Starmer-Smith.
8 Bill Beaumont, Charlie Faulkner and Alan Lewis.
9 Tane Norton (on the 1977 Lions tour to New Zealand).
10 Gloucester beat Moseley 17–6.
11 Ray (Chico) Hopkins (v England 1970); Clive Shell (v Australia 1973).
12 East Midlands and the Barbarians.

19   Home: Snooker 1

1 Ray Reardon was World Professional Champion; Cliff Wilson was World Amateur Champion. Both were born in Tredegar.
2 Jimmy van Rensberg of SA; Patsy Fagan of Ireland.
3 Eddie Sinclair of Scotland; Jim Rempe of USA.
4 Terry Griffiths (1st round); John Spencer (2nd round).
5 Jimmy White.
6 Australia, in 1975.
7 It was his first (and the game's) maximum 147 in competition (in the 1955 *News of the World* Tournament).
8 John Spencer, in 1977.
9 Joe Davis.
10 Ray Reardon.
11 Ray Reardon.
12 26. (13 reds plus 12 blacks = 97; then any of the higher colours will do.)

Gold Beaters

a) Bregawn; b) Captain John; c) Wayward Lad; d) Silver Buck; e) Ashley House.

20   Away 4

1 Table tennis.
2 Equestrian (show jumping and eventing); shooting.
3 Croquet. (The colours are the balls, and there are six hoops out, round a peg, and six hoops back.)
4 Curling.
5 David Bryant, in the World Indoor Bowls Championship.
6 Stock car racing.
7 Orienteering.
8 Paul Newman, the film star.
9 Marbles.

10 Golf (Walker Cup 1922; Ryder Cup 1927). Please forgive the misleading spelling in the question!

11 The Winter Olympics will be staged at Sarajevo, where Archduke Ferdinand was killed in 1914, thus precipitating the First World War.

12 Burleigh Three-Day Event – it's a water hazard.

21   One-minute Round 5

TEAM A

1 Tony Shaw.
2 Basketball.
3 Corbiere and Ben de Haan.
4 Burnley, Portsmouth, Chelsea, Derby County, Leeds United.
5 a) Warwickshire, b) Leicestershire, c) Kent.

TEAM B

1 Landsdowne Road.
2 Speedway.
3 Brian Fletcher (1973 and 1974); Tommy Stack (1977).
4 Innsbruck (1976); Sapporo (1972).
5 a) Lawn *Tennis* Association, b) World *Boxing* Council, c) World Professional *Billiards and Snooker* Association.

Which Game?

a) Croquet, b) polo, c) golf, d) lacrosse, e) baseball, f) shinty.

22   Home: Soccer 3

1 Terry Fenwick.
2 Ian McFaul.
3 Aston Villa, Nottingham Forest and Liverpool.
4 Paulo Rossi (for Italy v Brazil); Karl Heinz Rumenigge
   (for West Germany v Chile); Lazlo Kiss (for Hungary v
   El Salvador); Zbigniew Boniek (for Poland v Belgium).
5 Inter-Milan 1967 (won 2–1); Feyenoorde 1970 (lost
   2–1).
6 John McGovern.
7 Norman Hunter.
8 Arsenal (1933–4–5); Huddersfield Town (1924–5–6).
9 Ross Jenkins.
10 Bolton Wanderers.
11 Jairzinho.
12 Nottingham Forest.

23   Home: Cricket 2

1 Rohan Kanhai; Alvin Kallicharran; Deryck Murray;
   Lance Gibbs.
2 Fred Trueman, in 1964.
3 Viv Richards: he played for Antigua v Haiti in a 1974
   World Cup qualifying match.
4 John Edrich (replacement); Mike Denness (dropped
   captain).
5 Kent (1973 and 1976).
6 Stuart Surridge and Peter May.
7 Michael Holding of West Indies.
8 W. G. Grace.
9 Lancashire, in 1970.
10 Lindsay Hassett.
11 Ian Botham (on his debut) and Geoffrey Boycott.
12 They opened the batting for Sri Lanka in their country's
   first-ever Test Match.

24   Home: Golf 1

1 Peter Thomson and James Braid.
2 St Andrews, Scotland. Both are golf courses, and there are two others there, more famous perhaps – the 'Old' and the 'New'.
3 Doug Sanders and Jack Nicklaus: (Nicklaus won).
4 Gordon Brand Jnr.
5 Arnold Palmer.
6 Roberto de Vicenzo.
7 The US Masters (1968), won by Bob Goalby.
8 Bob Charles (1963).
9 Gary Player.
10 Severiano Ballesteros (1979); Gary Player (1974).
11 Tom Weiskopf and Johnny Miller.
12 Max Faulkner, in 1951.

British Open

1952: Bobby Locke; 1958: Peter Thomson; 1963: Bob Charles; 1969: Tony Jacklin; 1974: Gary Player; 1979: Severiano Ballesteros.

25   Home: Show Jumping

1 Anne Moore on Psalm.
2 Anneli Drummond-Hay (now Mrs Wucherpfennig).
3 First Boomerang; second Kerrygold.
4 Pele and Paul Darragh of Ireland.
5 Colonel Harry Llewellyn, on Foxhunter.
6 David Broome, in 1970.
7 Fritz Ligges.
8 Pat Smythe; Ann Moore.
9 Raimondo d'Inzeo (Gold); Piero d'Inzeo (Silver).
10 Pat Smythe, in 1956.
11 Hugo Simon on Gladstone.
12 Ann Moore: first; Alison Dawes (née Westwood): second.

26   Away 5

1 Night Nurse, the steeplechaser.
2 Hockey.
3 He was the Russian who scored the winning basket in the Olympic basketball final against USA – which, it was claimed, had been scored after time.
4 Table tennis (Men's Team Event).
5 Hungary.
6 Troon: it is the seventh hole on the course.
7 Badminton (at Badminton Hall).
8 Curling (to sweep the ice in front of the 'stone').
9 Norway.
10 Bowls.
11 Avery Brundage.
12 Tracy Austin.

27   One-minute Round 6

TEAM A

1 Brands Hatch.
2 Dennis Lillee.
3 Liverpool (1981–2–3); Nottingham Forest (1978–9).
4 a) squash, b) cricket.
5 a) Bobby Moore, b) Virginia Wade, c) John Dawes.

_____

TEAM B

1 Aintree Grand National course.
2 Geoffrey Boycott.
3 Cross-country skiing and shooting.
4 a) clay pigeon shooting, b) fencing.
5 a) Budge Rogers, b) Jocky Wilson, c) Daley Thompson.

28   Home: Athletics 3

1 Herb Elliot of Australia.
2 Ruth Fuchs.
3 Mary Stewart.
4 Lasse Viren (1972 and 1976).
5 Filbert Bayi of Tanzania.
6 Marita Koch.
7 Eamonn Coghlan.
8 Renate Stecher, in 1972.
9 Bill Nieder.
10 Long Jump (Gold); Pentathlon (Silver); 4 × 100-Metres Relay (Bronze).
11 Brendan Foster (Silver); David Black (Bronze).
12 Frank Clement and David Moorcroft.

29   Home: Horse Racing 2

1 Colin Magnier, in 1982.
2 Stan Mellor.
3 Brigadier Gerard.
4 Joe Mercer.
5 They were brother and sister: Freddie Head (the jockey), and Christine Head (the trainer).
6 To-Agori-Mou and Kings Lake.
7 Sceptre. (The Sceptre Stakes are run at Epsom.)
8 Little Owl (1st); Night Nurse (2nd).
9 Terry Biddlecombe and Bob Davies.
10 Nijinsky (1970); The Minstrel (1977).
11 Ron Barry in 1973 (with 125).
12 Nijinsky.

Derby Winners

1954: Never Say Die; 1957: Crepello; 1960: St Paddy; 1968: Sir Ivor; 1970: Nijinsky; 1972: Roberto; 1976: Empery; 1977: The Minstrel; 1983: Teenoso.

30   Home: Soccer 4

1 Peter Withe.
2 Bayern Munich.
3 El Salvador.
4 Aberdeen.
5 Fulham (1968); Luton Town (1969–70); Newcastle United (1971–5); Arsenal (1976–8).
6 Lato.
7 Anderlecht.
8 Aston Villa.
9 Leeds United, in 1975.
10 Stirling Albion (Annfield).
11 Manchester United. (Denis Law in 1964; Bobby Charlton in 1966; George Best in 1968).
12 Wolverhampton Wanderers, in 1958 and 1959.

31   Away 6

1 Golf: they are different types of competition.
2 Lacrosse.
3 The Greyhound Derby.
4 American (College) Football.
5 John Surtees, in motor cycling and motor racing.
6 The vault: she was fourth.
7 Ten Pin Bowling.
8 Heather Mackay.
9 Skiing – it's the downhill course at Lake Placid.
10 Volleyball.
11 Hanging on the rings, in a Men's Gymnastic routine.
12 Snooker.

32   One-minute Round 7

TEAM A

1 Brian Close (at 18).
2 First woman cox of the Oxford Boat Race crew.
3 Muhammed Ali and George Foreman (in Zaïre).
4 a) Alexander Zaitsev, b) Valery Borzov.
5 a) Argentina, b) Portugal, c) Spain.

TEAM B

1 Sir Gary Sobers.
2 Old Trafford, in 1970.
3 Muhammed Ali and Joe Frazier.
4 a) Smith, b) Hutton.
5 a) baseball, b) tennis, c) athletics.

Olympic Champion

Pommel horse; rings; vault; parallel bars; horizontal bars; floor exercises.

33   Home: Soccer 5

1 New Zealand; Algeria; Cameroon; Honduras; Kuwait.
2 Alan Ball, in 1966 (from Blackpool to Everton).
3 Daniel Bertoni: (Kempes scored 38 minutes and 105 minutes; Bertoni 115 minutes).
4 Terry Paine: (824 for Southampton and Hereford United).
5 Mario Zagalo: (he played for Brazil in 1958 and 1962; and was manager in 1970).
6 Danny Blanchflower.
7 Sir Stanley Matthews.
8 New York Cosmos.
9 Sheffield United.
10 Brian Clough: (200 goals in 219 games).
11 Steve Archibald (Spurs); Peter Withe (Aston Villa).
12 Arsenal.

34   Home: Rugby Union 2

1 All thirty players were sent off, seven minutes from time, for an unseemly punch-up!
2 Paul Ford of Gloucester; Mike Perry of Moseley.
3 Munster and Bridgend.
4 Jean-Pierre Romeu.
5 Bill Beaumont (1980); F. D. Prentice (1930).
6 Hugo Porta.
7 John Scott and Barry Nelms.
8 Andy Irvine.
9 Neil Bennett.
10 Ronald Thompson.
11 The Ranfurly Shield.
12 Richard Sharp.

35   Home: Darts

1 Keith Deller beat Eric Bristow.
2 Cliff Inglis.
3 Alan Glazier.
4 Ceri Morgan.
5 Tom Barrett.
6 Sweden.
7 Eric Bristow.
8 Treble 20, treble 17, bullseye.
9 Leighton Rees.
10 Stefan Lord.
11 John Lowe.
12 Harry Leadbetter.

Supporters' Club

a) Southampton or St Johnstone, b) West Ham United,
c) Luton Town, d) Swansea City, e) Everton, f) Arsenal,
g) Sheffield Wednesday.

36   Home: Boxing 2

1 Rocky Mattioli.
2 Henry Cooper.
3 Bunny Johnson, in 1975.
4 Leon Spinks and Sugar Ray Leonard.
5 Ken Buchanan, John H. Stracey and Maurice Hope.
6 Terry Downes and Paul Pender.
7 Jack Dempsey.
8 Jersey Joe Walcott.
9 Bob Foster: (Finnegan was knocked out in the 14th round.)
10 Alan Minter.
11 Dave Charnley.
12 Henry Armstrong.

37   Away 7

1 Netball.
2 Elena Mukhina of USSR.
3 Victor Barna.
4 Lawn Tennis.
5 The Oval, at Kennington.
6 Chris and Alan Old.
7 Oulton Park race circuit in Cheshire.
8 It starts at Putney; finishes at Mortlake.
9 Mandy Jones: road racing.
10 Ice-Dancing.
11 Archery.
12 Swimming (Duncan Goodhew); Figure Skating (Robin Cousins).

38   One-minute Round 8

TEAM A

1 Darts.
2 Millwall.
3 Somerset (John Player and Gillette); Essex (County Championship and Benson and Hedges Cup).
4 Swimming, Modern Pentathlon, Yachting.
5 a) Mexico, b) Munich, c) Tokyo.

TEAM B

1 Modern Pentathlon.
2 Charlton Athletic.
3 Old Belvedere and Leicester.
4 James Hunt, Barry Sheene, Peter Collins.
5 a) steeplechase, b) clay pigeon shooting, c) yachting.

39   Home: Soccer 6

1 Paolo Rossi of Italy, with 6.
2 Chelsea; AC Milan; West Ham; Spurs.
3 Uruguay.
4 Inverness Thistle and Falkirk.
5 Panathinaikos (1971); Inter-Milan (1972); Juventus (1973).
6 Brian and Jimmy Greenhoff for Manchester United, in 1977.
7 Di Stefano; Puskas (twice); Prati.
8 John Hollins (England); Dave Hollins (Wales).
9 Leeds United.
10 Feyenoord.
11 Tottenham Hotspurs, in 1963.
12 Plymouth Argyle.

40　　Home: Cricket 3

1　Old Trafford.
2　Dennis Amiss; Keith Fletcher; Zaheer Abbas.
3　Len Hutton.
4　Sussex.
5　Tony Lock.
6　Wilfred Rhodes.
7　Leicestershire.
8　Denis Compton, in 1947, with 18.
9　Rohan Kanhai.
10　Yorkshire.
11　Alan Knott.
12　Peter May (41 Tests).

Which County?

a) Worcestershire, b) Kent, c) Sussex, d) Gloucestershire,
e) Glamorgan, f) Warwickshire, g) Leicestershire.

41　　Home: Athletics 4

1　Sheila Carey (née Taylor).
2　Christine Benning (née Tranter).
3　Berwyn Price.
4　Thierry Vigneron of France, in 1981.
5　Emil Zatopek and Lass Viren.
6　Donna Hartley (née Murray).
7　Barbel Wockel (née Eckert); Romy Muller (née Schneider); Marlies Gohr (née Elsner).
8　Howard Payne (hammer); Rosemary Payne (discus).
9　Irena Szewinska (née Kirzenstein).
10　Pam Kilborn.
11　Bobby-Joe Morrow (1956); Valery Borzov (1972).
12　Chris Chataway and Chris Brasher.

I bring you a Message . . .

Riding; shooting; swimming; fencing; running.

42   Home: Tennis 2

1 Tracy Austin, in 1979 (aged 16).
2 Fred Stolle: (by McKinley in 1963, and by Emerson in 1964 and 1965).
3 Margaret Osborne (later du Pont).
4 Neale Fraser (1960); Alex Olmedo (1959).
5 Bobby Wilson and Mike Davies.
6 Vera Sukova, in 1962.
7 Maureen Connolly (1953); Margaret Court (1970).
8 Alex Metreveli and Olga Morozova.
9 Argentina.
10 Margaret Smith and Leslie Turner (1964); Margaret Court (née Smith) and Judy Tegart (1969); Kerry Reid and Wendy Turnbull (1978).
11 Kurt Neilson (1953 and 1955).
12 Angela Buxton (GB 1956); Darlene Hard (US 1957); Maria Bueno (Brazil 1958).

Wimbledon Finalist

1954: Drobny; 1956: Hoad; 1970: Newcombe; 1974: Connors.

43   One-minute Round 9

TEAM A

1 Brazil: (soccer stadium in Rio de Janeiro).
2 The hammer.
3 Henry Cooper (to March); Joe Bugner (to September); Jack Bodell (to December).
4 Marion Coakes on Stroller.
5 1974 – Evert; 1977 – Wade; 1978 – Navratilova.

TEAM B

1 South Africa (the rugby union stadium in Johannesburg).
2 Race Walking (20-kilometre walk).
3 Liverpool and Leeds United.
4 David Broome on Mister Softee.
5 1974 – Emerson Fittipaldi; 1976 – James Hunt; 1978 – Mario Andretti.

44   Home: Horse Racing 3

1 Auckland, New Zealand: (one of the top three races in the New Zealand calendar.
2 Quare Times (1955); Gay Trip (1970).
3 Arkle (1964–5–6); Fort Leney (1968).
4 Vaguely Noble.
5 Roberto: (1972 Benson and Hedges Gold Cup at York).
6 Fred Winter in 1961.
7 Ragusa (1963); Ribocco (1967); Ribero (1968); Boucher (1972).
8 Alleged.
9 Sir Gordon Richards, in 1952: (he did it every year from 1946–52).
10 Kentucky Derby, Belmont Stakes and Preakness Stakes.
11 Tommy Kinane (1978); Dessie Hughes (1979).
12 Tap on Wood.

45 Home: Rugby League

1 Widnes and Hull.
2 Hunslet (1979–80), Oldham (1981–2).
3 David Watkins, for Salford (1972–3, 1973–4).
4 Don Fox (for Wakefield Trinity against Leeds).
5 Neil Fox (with 6,276).
6 Sid Hynes (in 1971).
7 Lewis Jones (of Leeds) (Tally does not include friendly matches).
8 Leigh.
9 Widnes (1975–6–7).
10 Salford.
11 Eric Ashton.
12 Hull.

Olympic Teams

Ice hockey; soccer; volleyball; water polo; basketball; hockey; handball.

46 Home: Golf 2

1 Royal Lytham St Annes.
2 Arnold Palmer.
3 Jack Newton (Australia).
4 Severiano Ballesteros and Antonio Garrido.
5 Lou Graham (who lost by one shot).
6 Lee Trevino, in 1971.
7 Gary Player, in 1959.
8 Dai Rees, in 1957.
9 Peter Thomson and Kel Nagle.
10 Bobby Jones, in 1930.
11 Phil Rodgers of USA.
12 Walter Hagen, in 1922.

47   Home: Three-day Eventing

1 Eddie Boylan (Ireland 1965); Mark Todd (New Zealand 1980).
2 Bruce Davidson.
3 Captain Mark Phillips.
4 Ireland.
5 1st: HRH Princess Anne; 2nd: Debbie West; 3rd: Stewart Stevens.
6 Mary Gordon-Watson, on Cornishman, in 1970.
7 Derek Allhusen and Reuben Jones.
8 Kilbarry and Frank Weldon.
9 Janet Hodgson. (The team won a Bronze and she had her teeth in plaster for three months!)
10 Richard Meade on Laurieston.
11 Mary Gordon-Watson; Bridget Parker; Richard Meade; Mark Phillips.
12 Sheila Wilcox (1957–9).

48:   One-minute Round 10

TEAM A

1 Table tennis.
2 Peter Fleming.
3 Pole vault and triple jump.
4 Thomas Cup (men); Uber Cup (women).
5 a) Arthur, b) Diane or Rosalind, c) Lawrence.

TEAM B

1 Waterskiing.
2 Michael Lee.
3 Tottenham Hotspurs and Chelsea (in 1967).
3 Swaythling Cup (men); Corbillon Cup (women).
5 a) Alan, b) Ann, c) Bobby.

Playing Away

Huddersfield Town; Manchester City; Torino; Manchester United.

49   Home: Soccer 7

1 Malcolm Macdonald (Newcastle 1973, Arsenal 1978); Peter Osgood (Chelsea 1970, Southampton 1976); Brian Talbot (Ipswich 1978, Arsenal 1979).
2 Billy Meredith, who played from 1895–1920.
3 Brian Clough (Notts Forest and Derby County); Herbert Chapman (Huddersfield Town and Arsenal).
4 Honved.
5 Brentford, Chelsea, Bradford Park Avenue, Fulham.
6 In England in 1966.
7 Liverpool (1965); Chelsea (1970); Sunderland (1973).
8 Pat Jennings (Spurs) scored against Alex Stepney (Manchester United).
9 Tottenham Hotspurs, in 1961.
10 Rotherham United.
11 Benfica.
12 Johnny Haynes.

50   Home: Athletics 5

1 Irena Szewinska (200-Metres, 1968; 400-Metres, 1976); Betty Cuthbert (200-Metres, 1956; 400-Metres, 1964).
2 Henry Rono (*1st*) and Mike Musyoki (*2nd*).
3 Grazyna Rabjztyn of Poland.
4 Janis Lusis of USSR.
5 1500-Metres.
6 Bob Mathias (1948 and 1952).
7 Andrea Lynch (100-Metres).
8 Vladislav Kozakiewicz of Poland.
9 Marjorie Jackson (1952); Betty Cuthbert (1956).
10 Al Oertèr (discus).
11 Ralph Boston.
12 Randy Matson.

51   Home: Judo

1 Christine Child.
2 Tokyo, in 1964.
3 Shozo Fujii.
4 Light-heavy (80–93 kilos); Welter-weight (or Light-middleweight 63–70 kilos).
5 Anton Geesink, in 1961.
6 Angelo Parisi and Brian Jacks.
7 Keith Remfry.
8 Sergei Novikov of USSR.
9 Neil Adams.
10 Wilhelm Ruska.
11 Jane Bridge.
12 Karen Briggs.

52   Home: Boxing 3

1 Kevin Finnegan.
2 Tony Sibson.
3 Leon and Michael Spinks.
4 Len Harvey.
5 Bob Fitzsimmons, in the 1890s.
6 Roberto Duran.
7 Jimmy Price.
8 Jimmy Braddock.
9 Wilfred Benitez.
10 Rocky Marciano.
11 Teofilio Stevenson.
12 Ingemaar Johannson.

53   Away 8

1 Larissa Latynina (9 Gold, 5 Silver, 4 Bronze).
2 A motor racing circuit in New York State.
3 Hugh Porter.
4 Weightlifting.
5 Golfers: it is the World Amateur Team Championship.

120

6 Double sculls, and Men's Eights.
7 Handball.
8 Darts: (20 is situated between 5 and 1; double 16 is between 7 and 8).
9 Squash.
10 Mike Hailwood, in 1961.
11 He was a double international for two countries, playing rugby for England, and cricket for South Africa.
12 Babe Zaharias (née Didrikson).

Decathlon Champion

100-Metres; long jump; high jump; shot put; discus; pole vault; javelin; 400-Metres; 110-Metres hurdles; 1500-Metres.

54   One-minute Round 11

TEAM A

1 Edinburgh: scene of the famous professional sprint race.
2 Diving.
3 Ivan Mauger and Ove Fundin.
4 Ken Matthews (1964); Don Thompson (1960).
5 a) West Indies (cricket); b) Spain (soccer); c) Northern Ireland (motor sport).

TEAM B

1 Ascot.
2 Squash.
3 West Indies and Australia (cricket).
4 Jaroslav Drobny and Jan Kodes.
5 a) Brand's Hatch; b) Isle of Man TT circuit; c) The Oval.

55   Home: Soccer 8

1 Notts County (founded 1862).
2 Martin Peters (from West Ham to Spurs).
3 Flamengo.
4 Terry Bly (52 for Peterborough in 1960–1).
5 Hungary.
6 Newcastle United and Tottenham Hotspurs.
7 Manchester United (1956–7 season).
8 Northampton Town.
9 Port Vale.
10 Ron Springett and Peter Bonetti.
11 Stanley Mortensen, in 1953.
12 Uwe Seeler.

56   Home: Badminton

1 The Devlins: Father (Frank) got six, and daughter (Judy, now Hashman) ten.
2 Eva Twedberg (1968 and 1971).
3 Thomas Kihlstrom (of Sweden).
4 Rudy Hartono (1978); Flemming Delfs (1979).
5 Tony Jordan.
6 Norah Perry and Jane Webster.
7 Hiroe Yuki of Japan: 1974 and 1975.
8 Jamie Paulson (Men's Singles).
9 Helen Troke.
10 Ray Stevens and Mike Tredgett.
11 Kitty McKane (Mrs Godfree).
12 Gold: Margaret Beck (Lockwood); Silver: Gillian Perrin (Gilks); Bronze: Margaret Boxall (Allen).

Doubles Partners

1961 and 1962: Karen Susman (née Hantz); 1965: Maria Bueno; 1967, 1968, 1970, 1971 and 1973: Rosemary Casals; 1972: Betty Stove; 1979: Martina Navratilova.

57   Home: Rugby Union 3

1 Because Cardiff had scored a try and Bridgend had not.
2 Richard Sharp, in 1963.
3 Edinburgh Academicals.
4 Ken Jones.
5 All five countries shared the title.
6 Keith Jarrett, against England.
7 Bobby Windsor, Graham Price, Charlie Faulkner.
8 Colin Meads of New Zealand.
9 Bridgend.
10 Canada.
11 Lucien Mias.
12 France.

58   Home: Athletics 6

1 1948, in London.
2 Irina Press, in 1964.
3 Judy Vernon (1974); Lorna Booth (1978).
4 Verona Elder.
5 Paavo Nurmi.
6 Scotland.
7 Vladimir Kuts.
8 Steve Ovett (1500-Metres).
9 Judy Peckham.
10 Wyomia Tyus (100-Metres: 1964 and 1968).
11 Tatyana Kazankina.
12 Glenn Davis of USA: 1956 and 1960.

59   Home: Horse Racing 4

1 Dahlia (1973 and 1974).
2 Fred Rimell (ESB: 1956; Nicolaus Silver: 1961; Gay
  Trip: 1970; Rag Trade: 1976).
3 Pinza (1953).
4 Red Alligator (1968); Red Rum (1973 and 1974).

5 Each won the Champion Hurdle three times in succession.
6 Vincent O'Brien.
7 Dunfermline.
8 Charlotte Brew, in 1977.
9 Geraldine Rees, in 1982.
10 Manchester: (the course is now closed).
11 Dick Francis, the thriller writer.
12 John Henry.

Seven Events

100-Metres hurdles; shot put; high jump; long jump; 200-Metres; javelin; 800-Metres.

60   Home: Snooker 2

1 Doug Mountjoy (13–12, 2nd round); Jimmy White (16–15, Semi-final).
2 Wales.
3 Walter Donaldson.
4 Cliff Thorburn, in 1979.
5 Tommy Murphy.
6 Tony Knowles (beaten by Cliff Thorburn); Alex Higgins (beaten by Steve Davis).
7 Patsy Fagan.
8 36 (15 reds, 15 blacks, and 6 colours).
9 Gary Owen (1963 and 1966).
10 Cliff Thorburn (1983 and 1980); Perrie Mans (1978).
11 Alex Higgins, in 1972.
12 Willie Thorne, with 25.

61 One-minute Round 12

TEAM A

1 Badminton.
2 Trent Bridge.
3 Maria Bueno and Alex Olmedo.
4 John Curry and Dorothy Hamill.
5 1973: Bob Stokoe; 1975: Ron Greenwood; 1977: Tommy Docherty.

TEAM B

1 Rifle shooting.
2 Bob Willis.
3 Jacques Anquetil and Eddy Merckx.
4 1958: Sweden; 1962: Czechoslovakia; 1970: Italy.
5 1962: Perth, W. Australia; 1970: Edinburgh; 1974: Christchurch, New Zealand.